STORIES OF FAITH

STORIES OF FAITH

John Finney

British and Foreign Bible Society
Stonehill Green, Westlea, Swindon, SN5 7DG, England

Unless otherwise stated, quotation from the Bible are from the Good News Bible, published by the Bible Societies/HarperCollins Publishers Ltd UK

© American Bible Society, New York 1966, 1971, 1976 and 1992.

A catalogue record for this book is available from the British Library
ISBN 0564 087459

Printed in Great Britain by Redwood Books

Cover design by Adept Design, Aylsham, Norwich

Bible Societies exist to provide resources for Bible distribution and use. The British and Foreign Bible Society (BFBS) is a member of the United Bible Societies, an international partnership working in over 180 countries. Their common aim is to reach all people with the Bible, or some part of it, in a language they can understand and at a price they can afford. Parts of the Bible have now been translated into over 2,000 languages. Bible Societies aim to help every church at every point where it uses the Bible. You are invited to share in this work by your prayers and gifts. The Bible Society in your country will be very happy to provide details of its activity.

INTRODUCTION

After Finding Faith Today

- What happens when somebody comes to faith?
- Do "converts" all have the same experience?
- Does our evangelism build on reality or is it based on a few melodramatic stories?
- Do we force people 's experience into a rather stilted theological strait-jacket?

Evangelism is one of the main efforts of the Church but is it built on the sand of fantasy or the rock of reality? In the Decade of Evangelism we need to know, or we shall waste much Christian effort and money fruitlessly.

For many years I had been fascinated by the ways in which people come to faith. In the early 1980s I did some research which produced surprising results, but it was too amateurish to be able to erect a policy of mission on its findings. However, it made me want to find out more.

Eventually I described the need to the Evangelism Committee of the British Council of Churches. They decided that it was such an important subject that they would give their backing to a project which looked into the subject with much greater rigour. That was December 1989. They set up an interdenominational group to monitor the work with representatives from the Roman Catholic, Brethren, Anglican, Methodist, URC and House churches. All denominations realized they were equally ignorant in this area.

Together with the Bible Society a full-time professional researcher, Pam Hanley, was employed to do the fieldwork, which involved interviewing over 500 adults from all denominations who had made a public profession of faith (in baptism, confirmation, etc.) in the previous year.

Based on Pam's results, I wrote *Finding Faith Today* (FFT). I should say that FFT does not include all of Pam's work but this book gives me the opportunity of including some facts which have only been published in her research findings.

During the time we were doing the research, two significant things happened. The first was the adoption, by most churches, of the Decade of Evangelism which has highlighted the importance of mission. Secondly, the recession and the financial squeeze hit the churches (and all voluntary societies) very hard indeed. This resulted in churches becoming cost-conscious. This involved finding out how effective the actions of the Church are. Evangelism has to show that it is worthwhile and effective.

FFT was published in October 1992. An Archbishop, a Cardinal and the President of the Free Church Council were at the launch! I had a lowering feeling that it could only go downhill after that, but the book was well reviewed and a flood of invitations came in from all parts of England as well as from Scotland and Wales to give presentations of the material. To date I have done over forty.

In doing so I learnt a great deal. As part of each presentation I read the story of one of the respondents without comment and then asked the audience to talk amongst themselves about the story and what they had learnt from it.

Several things stood out:

(a) Most of the people at the presentations were Christian leaders. Very few of them had ever thought they could learn anything from such stories. They were to thank God for, and to be wondered at, and to repeat in sermons, but not to learn from.

(b) Many of these Christian leaders had no knowledge of the faith journeys of the people in their own congregation. How had that "pillar of the kirk" become a Christian? What early experiences of church had led to the problems which Mrs X was going through? What seemed to be obvious questions had not been asked.

(c) Many Christian leaders were merely experimenting with evangelism, hoping that they would find the instant answer which would convert the population. Hence there were waves of interest in one thing after another: "Evangelism Explosion", power evangelism, Willowcreek, friendship evangelism, evangelism through worship, the catechumenate.

Yet the evidence is under our noses. It makes sense to ask the people who have recently become Christians through the ministry of a church what human and spiritual means the Holy Spirit has used to bring them to faith. It may be that the Holy Spirit will bring others to faith in the same way as these people. Too often churches evangelize strenuously in one direction while God brings people into the church in a very different way. For years one congregation had run a vigorous and time-consuming house-to-house visiting programme, but research showed that only one person had come into the life of the church through that means – and there was even some doubt about him! But the church had grown, largely through people being asked "Would you like to come to church with me next Sunday?"

There is something in us which wants "heroic" evangelism which takes much time and money. This may be less effective than simply befriending another human being and introducing them to our group or congregation and then to Christ. Is it because we prefer "technological evangelism" which uses the latest gadgetry to manoeuvre people into the Kingdom rather than the love which our Lord used?

(d) People at the presentations began by talking together about the story of another human being. But it did not end there. Before long they began to compare that story with others they had come across – "Glenda did not come to Christ like that...", "That's just what happened to my uncle". If I gave them an extra minute or two they began to compare the story with their own – "that woman had exactly the same pattern of life as I had". *In fact one of the best ways of encouraging people to testify to how God has worked in their own lives is to begin with the experience of someone else.*

(e) A practical footnote: it was very noticeable that people engaged much more with the story when it was read aloud than when they read it from a sheet of paper. The human voice gives warmth and realism. If you are using this book in a group, ask someone to read the story aloud and then discuss it. This is particularly important when you come to the stories which have very few comments or questions.

The power of the story

Before the written word was the spoken word.

Anthropologists say that members of primitive communities communicated through stories. They were told around the fire at night or to the children as part of their upbringing. Each tribe had its own set of epics which told their own history in mythological form. The storyteller has been an honoured member of the community from ancient times onwards. The Norwegian skald told his stories to the twanging of his harp and recounted the great deeds of their Viking forebears and the misty regions of the gods which lay about them. The present was joined with the past through long genealogies which told of "Caelic, son of Breca, son of Getwulf...". The words of the stories were accurately handed down with extraordinary precision, each skald dependent upon his predecessors from whom he had learnt the narratives.

The Old Testament is full of stories, genealogies, accounts of the deeds of the great times when Moses brought the people of Israel out of Egypt. However, the God of Israel is not seen in a vague heroic pantheon but in majestic reality, leading, judging, and loving his people on their pilgrimage.

It is a truism to say that Jesus taught in stories: the farmer ... the banker ... the ruler ... the spendthrift ... the housewife ... the fisherman ... the civil servant. They all appear in the gospels. He who knows what is in the heart knows that stories stick. Exhortation becomes wearisome but stories excite.

Something that is often overlooked is that Jesus told stories about people, not about things or ideas. So should we. The tabloid press have always known this – "Petite brunette, 39-year-old housewife...". Surprisingly, advertisers are only just beginning to realize that our attention is grasped if we become hooked by a story. The country became intrigued by the trivial romance of the *Nescafé* couple. We often do not know if Jesus' stories were based on actual, specific events and personalities. Had a traveller to Jericho recently been beaten up? Had an unjust steward defrauded his employer just before his dismissal? If so Jesus' listeners would have recognized the incident he was describing and their attention would have been even more firmly focused on his words. We know that Jesus alluded to current events, as when he mentioned the eighteen people killed in the disaster at Siloam.

The nature of a parable is significant. It is not a moral tale to illustrate a point. It has a validity of its own. That is why parables are not easy to preach from. Similarly, if a joke has to be explained it loses its point. A preacher is unwise if he labours the "meaning" of a parable story because each one speaks to different people in a different way.

Somewhat old-fashioned biblical expositors attempted to find a single meaning to each parable, but they were unable to agree on what that single meaning was. Most Christians too have experienced finding new meanings to well-known parables.

What is true for you in the story is true. Each person reading this book will pick up different things from each story just as we don't all buy the same things when we go into a shop.

Stories require hearers. The skald, or the Old Testament prophet, had to have an audience. A joke told to yourself is not much fun, nor is the story of what happened to you in town the other day. A story is something which moves from the experience of one person to that of another, whether it is a New Testament parable or a story about a Scotsman, an Irishman, and an Englishman.

Stories need to be told. If we talk scandal, then the intimacy of a person-to-person conversation makes it more conspiratorial. Otherwise it is more satisfying to tell a story to a group and when you've got their attention to hear encouraging noises such as "Ahh", "Well I never", "Go on", "What happened then". Jesus' stories sometimes held thousands enthralled.

Stories are not necessarily lengthy. The parable of the mustard seed is only 43 words long. But, no matter how long or short a story is, it always conveys a picture. The picture in the speaker's mind is conveyed to us. Often this is best done with a few brush-strokes rather than by a long discourse.

In this book we are dealing with what happened to individuals. A personal story transfers the reality of one person's experience to another. The story which grips is the one with which the hearer can identify. That is why stories about "The operation I had last year" are boring, unless you have had the same illness yourself. Hence a story about someone like yourself is more engaging than about someone with a very different background. Stories of wonderful conversions far overseas do not grip like the stories of people who could be living next door.

Jesus used stories of everyday life because people could identify with them.

♦

Proverbs is a rich source of wisdom which comes from the heart of a storytelling society. There are constant references to the power of spoken words:

"A good person's words are a fountain of life, but a wicked person's words hide a violent nature." (10.11)

"A good person's words are like pure silver; a wicked person's ideas are worthless." (10.2)

"Proud fools talk too much; the words of the wise protect them." (14.3)

"A wise, mature person is known for his understanding. The more pleasant his words, the more persuasive he is." (16.21)

"An honest answer is a sign of true friendship." (24.26)

"Gossip is so tasty! How we love to swallow it!" (26.22)

◆

Narrative theology

In the past theologians have tended to see statements as being much more important than stories, whether in the Scriptures or the creeds. But much of the Bible is made up of narrative. Indeed nearly all credal statements are based on narrative.

To say "Jesus Christ died for our sins" is a statement of the doctrine of the atonement, but the atonement stems from the story of the crucifixion. Thus many narratives in the Bible are clearly factual but have a purpose much deeper than a history book. They may indeed be "true to life" in a much more subtle way than just recording what happened.

To be over concerned about the factual basis of some stories may cause you to miss the point entirely. The validity of the stories of Jonah or Job rests upon the deeper truths they convey, not on the accuracy of the details of the events described. Whether they are seen as fact or parable makes no difference to their significance.

There are also some non-western theologians who would say that the western concern with the "fact" has meant that Europeans and Americans often miss the meaning behind the fact.

◆

How to use this book to the full

(a) Treat each story with seriousness. There is a danger in thinking that stories are essentially light-weight compared with "solid teaching" and so we do not learn as much as we might. Jesus did not make that mistake.

(b) A group learns more from a story than an individual, because each member brings their experience to bear upon it. So use it with other people if possible.

(c) Let a story resonate. It takes time to realize its full significance. In a group, allow people time to talk about what the story says to them. If this is very different from what another person thinks, so much the better. If you are reading the book by yourself, do not give yourself indigestion by reading one story after another without thinking about each one carefully.

(d) Be aware of the human side of the story as well as the spiritual. Christians can sometimes be so eager to get to the "spiritual point" that they fail to notice the ordinary human happenings which have also been significant.

(e) Do not try to force the story to say more than it does. For example, do not try to find a point at which the person "became a Christian" because often there is no such obvious point. Allow them to say what they do say and not what we want them to say. (Editing of the stories has been kept to an absolute minimum in the light of this. In some cases this may lead to a certain amount of ambiguity, but the essence of each story should be clear.)

(f) If possible read the person's words aloud in a group.

(g) Notice how vividly people put things. This can spark ideas in our own minds.

(h) Think if there are scriptural parallels which illuminate the story. There are many which could have been included in this book, but it is more helpful and rewarding if you discover your own.

(i) There are questions at the end of each section, but if the story sparks other questions in your mind, address them and scrap mine!

Hannah

DEATH WISH

Hannah had planned her suicide for over a year:

> partly looking forward to dying – partly a great fear of it ... I had almost promised myself to do it. It seemed to be the only way out.
>
> I had the day planned.

She had been driven to this extremity by a sense of being

> lost with everything – killing myself to get rid of guilt and shame
>
> there were few periods when life has been worth living – really "nice".

At this stage she was 39 years old and "desperate". She "telephoned the local vicar" (getting the phone number from *Thompson's Directory* – the number "popped out of the book under 'Places of worship' ").

> I visited the manse two or three times in two days. Another new convert was there – after this time I became a Christian.

Hannah says in a matter-of-fact way:

> If I hadn't decided I would be dead.

She had been brought up with very little Christian background. Her parents had a "very negative" attitude to the Christian faith. She had hardly any contact with the church during childhood (except going to Church of England schools which she said had "little or no effect").

She had not watched Christian films, read Christian books or listened to Christian speakers. She had a vague interest in "Buddhism and philosophy" and found the whole Christian message difficult to believe in. She was single, a typist and despairing.

The telephone call caused a shift in her thinking:

> I had expected to meet an old geyser – but he was a young, friendly person who answered the phone. He was friendly and welcoming.

She also had a rapid change in her view of God. Before this encounter:

> I hated God. I believed there was someone there – but he was a holy person – and that was the reason for hating him.

Her conversion gave her

> a sense of hope. Jesus made the pieces fit together – he is in control. Also I was loved and wanted in the church and in the family

though she was well aware that at first she also wanted to be:

> less involved with the church while I was still screwed up.

Hannah also realizes that she still has difficulties in the "whole area of trust", both in her relationship with God and other people:

> I am still learning to trust God. The male/father figure draws out *anger*. I try to dare him – by putting him to the test. The fact of God's love is still sinking in.

> I met real people who were not sharing rubbish and so I felt safe to share myself.

It was not difficult to decide which church to go to:

> I had just been converted through the vicar so I went to his church.

(Hannah also says that she goes to Baptist and Roman Catholic churches as well as the Church of England.)

She found going to church "quite difficult". Before her conversion she "didn't like churches":

> I had problems with previous occult involvement and "voices" yet I was able to join in the singing, worship and teaching – but problems arose when I wanted a deeper involvement.

> I had an inner peace during these times – the voices shut up.

She also knew that her conversion had made her "much more outgoing".

When the interviewer asked her about her "out-of-the-ordinary experiences which you would describe as religious in some way", she said she would rather not talk about them because they were

"out of body" – occult type

though now as a Christian she had experiences of hearing "lovely 'words' from God" which "encourage for a time – then they get lost".

She found the preparation for confirmation very helpful. The service itself she described as "very worthwhile" but:

I was very frightened – but it was a seal of conversion, of God's work.

♦

There are many points which might be taken up from Hannah's story – the sense of lostness and extreme guilt, the consciousness of a guiding hand, the encounter with the church, the occult past, the masculinity of God, etc.

However, one question could be tackled:

♦ We know little about Hannah's past which seems to have led to a deep self-loathing and lack of trust in people. How common is this general lack of belief in oneself and others, and how does Christ respond to it?

♦ Are there biblical examples which can be helpful? You may like to see what can be learnt from Romans 7 and 8.

Annette

THE FEMALE NICODEMUS

Spiritually all was set fair for Annette.

She went to Sunday School very regularly from the age of 8 to 13. The Church of England primary school's expression of Christianity still gives her:

a nice warm feeling when I think what it was like.

She also found the Anglican Prayer Book she was given had lots of "very comforting, standard prayers".

In her secondary school she belonged to the Christian Fellowship until she was 13 and found the Bible "fascinating", though she confessed that she did not understand it!

The difficulty she had at 13 stemmed from moving house:

Didn't like [my] parent's new church because it was high.

The change was spiritually damaging. She began to go to church irregularly and eventually stopped going almost altogether for many years.

However, a strange incident happened when she was 18 and she felt "directed strongly to do something". She was working in a residential hotel but living elsewhere:

Had a Baptist minister's wife (mid–70s) staying and I was very fond of her. One morning [I] woke up and had to go straight to [the] hotel. She was on the floor in a state of collapse. I was driven – just had to be there. She was a devout Christian and we had a strong bond.

Annette trained as a nurse and still experienced the same sensitivity to situations:

When I was nursing I was aware that the intuitive feel for patients and people was very helpful. But it disappears if you're stressed and uptight.

Like many, the business of leaving school, starting a job, carving out a career, and getting married pushed God out of her mind. Work was particularly important for her:

> I had decided to be a career woman as I had been told that I would have no kids.

Annette came to a turning point when she was 33. Things began to change:

> I had my first child and moved to a community where I felt I belonged – we only moved a mile but it was totally different. Had no strong friendships in neighbourhood so met people every day who were going to church. I would creep into church but wouldn't let anyone see me – would have ruined my image.

It was not an easy time. When she was asked what things were happening in her life, she answered:

> becoming a parent – saw I had responsibilities to child. Had very bad post-natal depression. Dragged round to the odd service and put off by sermon, e.g. "should never turn to God just because you are in trouble" – directed at me.

> I was crazy, mixed up. Supposed to be on a high after having a baby and wasn't – seeking help and consolation to get me through that. But also very grateful that I had this lovely, whole little being.

Fortunately she met someone who could help her – the vicar's wife:

> she befriended me at a time when I needed it and accepted my incorrigible behaviour. ("You are on our prayer list" – me: "How long will it take to work?") She didn't give up....

Not all Christians were so helpful:

> Had a friend at work who was utterly horrible but went to church – I couldn't go to that church whilst she was there.

She joined a

> strong mother and toddler group – strong leader who is a very committed Christian.

The vicar and his wife were clearly still important:

> they have a young family and are realistic ... they knew what I was going through. They made it more welcoming than the old vicar who could never remember your name....

She started going to church regularly:

> It felt right to do so – I was ready to do so.

However, she found going to church "very difficult". When we asked her why she said:

> People I knew who went were very good about faith and talking about it. I never felt I would be (still am not really). Embarrassment of kids – e.g. taking bite out of courgettes at Harvest. Not knowing when to sit/stand. Believed I couldn't wear trousers and I hate skirts.... Feel a fraud as I feel others there have a lot to give and I'm still absorbing.

Eventually Annette got confirmed:

> Had always wanted to do it. Had taken me 27 years to decide.... Never felt good enough to be confirmed and classes made me realize it didn't matter. Felt I had to be perfect....

She was surprised by her own feelings at the time of the confirmation. She had not expected a spiritual experience:

> It was so important to me and I'd achieved something I'd always wanted to do ... it was nice afterwards 'cos kids came to be blessed at first communion and [my] husband supported me though he'd have nowt to do with it. Didn't feel a thing when hands were laid on me but felt strongly guided....

Since returning to church on a regular basis, it had taken her eight years before she felt ready for confirmation.

◆

> ◆ Annette looks back on the move to a new church when she was 13 as pushing her faith underground – although she continued to pray every day. Are we aware of many people like Annette?

♦ Annette was a female Nicodemus: coming to Christ but afraid of anyone seeing her. The rest of her story shows she is still rather fearful and conscious of her image. How can we help such people?

♦ Do you think the vicar actually said that people should not turn to God in trouble, or was it Annette's depression which made her think she heard it? Those undergoing the misery of depression often feel that everything is directed at them and hear words in their most accusatory form. Do we help such people sensitively?

♦ Notice the list of different things which put Annette off going to church – the expertise of more mature Christians, difficulties with lively young children – and a mistaken belief in how she thought one should dress. Are there similar off-putting elements in your church?

♦

Steve

BRIDGING THE GAP

One in five of the people who had made a personal profession of faith had had virtually no Christian upbringing. Steve was one of them. His family had "no religion", he never went to church or Sunday School as a youngster. His experience of the Christian faith at school "had little or no effect" on him. He never prayed, had no sense of guilt, and thought "not much" about God. He had never been inside a church. He never read the Bible. He describes his frame of mind as "happy" – indeed he was an archetypal "happy pagan".

But he watched Christian TV programmes and films, and he had Christian friends:

I worked with them and this lady was talking about God all the time.

It appears that no other factor was involved, Steve had just left school at 16 and started as a farm worker. Just about this time of transition he was invited to a Christian group and was converted straight away:

I was having a Bible study and I liked what I heard and I was saved that night.

The Bible had gripped him. He does not explain what part, but it (and his Christian friends) made a profound impression on him. He started going to church and has thoroughly thrown himself into its life.

What had it been like to step straight into a church environment from a totally non-church background? He described it as "quite easy":

> my friends go – made to feel at home.

Christians sometimes over-emphasize the cultural gap between themselves and the community and bemoan the difficulty which people experience in church. The research showed time and again that entering a church was quite easy provided they were taken along by a friend.

It had been a revelation for Steve:

> It's good. You learn a lot and the people are nice.

The church had not made it easy for him for

> I got saved the same night as I made the declaration:

> The person who saved me told me I had to tell others what I had done (i.e. made a commitment)

Since that time Steve has whole-heartedly entered church life:

> attending church once a week, and prayer meetings, house group meeting, youth group.

Indeed he says he would "like to be more involved. Nothing stops me". Like other people who came from right outside the orbit of the church he became even more addicted to churchgoing than those who had gone occasionally.

When he is asked about the change which becoming a Christian had made in his life he gave an apparently puzzling answer (which makes a great deal of sense when you think about it):

> It has made me hold my tongue a lot more.

> It has made me talk a lot more.

It was at a Bible study that he became a Christian and the Bible is still his first love. He reads it "several times a week" and it is "very" important to him. The youth group was important to him because:

> they got me to read and find the writers of the Bible.

♦

♦ Is a Bible study group for church people alone – or for non-Christians as well? Steve's story (and he is not alone) suggests that such groups can be directly evangelistic – even to someone like Steve with next to no Christian background.

♦ Do we keep the riches of the Scriptures away from people because "they will not understand it"? Do we feel that "the Bible is for teaching not evangelism"?

♦ The Church often tries to put fences round the "means of grace" making them inaccessible to those outside the church. Is this another case of this?

Kath

SET UPRIGHT AGAIN

Kath's description of her spiritual journey gives the impression of someone who was running smoothly through life until she felt that she had been derailed and needed to be put back on the track.

Kath is now 33, a teacher, married and working full time. She was brought up in a Christian home, went to Sunday School and church until she was 14 but then she stopped going because

I got bogged down with loads of homework.

Few incidents from her childhood meant much to her spiritually, though she was very moved by Robert Powell's portrayal of Jesus in *Jesus of Nazareth*. She was also taken to a Billy Graham rally:

...but I found that a bit frightening – everybody seemed to be in a kind of trance! I felt very uncomfortable there and was glad to get away.

She stopped going to church apart from once a year, though she never considered that she wasn't a Christian.

Then two incidents took place close together:

> When I went to midnight mass about two years ago I felt an uncanny peace come over me whilst in the church. I can't really describe how I felt.

> About two years ago I had a miscarriage. The whole experience knocked me about badly. I felt empty and unconsolable. No family, doctors or friends could help me. I turned to God for help in desperation, and from then I gradually recovered. I felt it was nothing short of a miracle. I went from being desolate to feeling human again. I shall be eternally grateful to God for healing my grief – as I am convinced he did.

She began to go to her local Anglican church regularly. It was "very easy":

> The people at my church are very friendly and made me very welcome. I look forward to going.

This led to a public commitment:

> About a year later [after the miscarriage] I was confirmed. I felt I owed God my loyalty and devotion, but more than that, I now felt I wanted to know him more and make him more part of my life. I only wished I had turned to God sooner. Now I trust that he will control my life for the best.

Like many others her view of God changed:

> Before: somebody that was powerful, but distant and unapproachable.

> After: somebody who loves and cares for you and of whom you can ask anything.

And like many others she feels more accepting of herself:

> I feel more confident and secure. It has made me realize that I can now be myself, for God loves me for what I am. It has given me peace of mind and the confidence that God will direct me through life to do his will.

◆

Kath was not alone in describing the devastating effect of a miscarriage. Do our churches give sufficient support during pregnancy, e.g.

♦ is the same support given to parents, and other members of the family, when someone miscarries, as there is when a baby dies? Are there proper funeral arrangements or other means of recognizing the loss of a human life?

♦ is there prayer support during pregnancy? Many churches have some form of thanksgiving service after a child is born. Do we need the equivalent in prayer during the anxious weeks leading up to the birth?

♦ is there help (especially during a first pregnancy) in enabling parents to come to terms with their responsibility in caring for and bringing up a child?

Shelley

THE POWER OF TESTIMONY

Shelley is a 20-year-old trainee nurse who was brought up as a Christian. She clearly had a good, solid Methodist grounding in the faith. She was never conscious of a time when she was not a Christian.

In one way Shelley is unusual. When we started the research project we expected more people to be influenced by Christian literature and other media. What we discovered was that few people had found them to be significant. Shelley is one of the exceptions, but what is most interesting is *what* she found helpful. It was stories about people which had captured her imagination and which she remembered. This was also true of nearly everyone else who had found books and the media helpful. She lists:

The Cliff Richard book, *Jesus, Me and You*, a TV documentary on Martin Luther King, the film *Jesus of Nazareth*, books about Mother Teresa (which she had read at school), *Joseph and the Amazing Technicolor Dreamcoat*, TV documentaries relating to the poor – good examples (also *Ghandi*).

As a nurse Shelley tries to

> base my life on service to God

and she has found her faith

> has taught me to be more confident about myself

She was confirmed at the age of 19:

> I was moving away to start nursing and was a member of the church for a long time so wanted to make my public commitment in front of people who knew me.

She had found the preparation in a small group of three "very worthwhile", though importantly she had wanted more time

> ♦ discussing the role of a Christian in today's life – it's a big jump from being an undecided Christian to a firm, declared one: it needs regular clarifying as to what that means.

> ♦ Shelley found stories about significant people very important to her. Other people had found *The Life of St Bernadette*, and a biography of C S Lewis helpful. Very few mentioned books of Christian teaching as being important. Does this mean that we should concentrate on getting these types of biographical books and videos into the public libraries, on our church bookstalls and be giving them as presents to our family and friends?

> ♦ Should we encourage publishers to produce material which can feed this need? They need especially to think of those like Sandra who are concerned for the world and so the stories about people who help the poor and raise social issues could be of particular importance.

> ♦ Shelley wanted more discussion of how the gospel related to her everyday life. All the ethical issues raised by her nursing training could cause a major gap in her understanding of the faith. Do churches help people to deal with these often controversial issues sufficiently? If not, how is it best done? If help isn't given, the church isn't equipping Christians to be confident in their witness to the world.

John

KICKING IN THE WALLS

John was brought up in a Baptist family and was made to go to church twice on Sundays:

> I was forced to be involved even in choir after my voice broke. Then I stopped altogether because I felt I was being made a fool of.

Despite going to church, there was not much individual commitment. He read the Bible "seldom or never" and "didn't think about it". The only thing about church he enjoyed were some of the Salvation Army services he attended when he was on holiday.

John rejected all profession of faith. For about thirty years he professed "no religion". As he says:

> Religion – I couldn't credit it

Though surprisingly he still had positive memories of the church:

> It was a friendly place to go where your children could go to be with people of similar values

He would argue against the Christian faith:

> I liked to "wooden spoon" it to get people going.

Then on 7 July 1989 he heard of the death of a close friend:

> We had been friends for nine years in the armed forces in some peculiar situations where we had to rely on each other quite heavily.

It had a big effect. John described his mood as

> very angry and very frustrated.
>
> For two days I walked around kicking the walls. Then I went to a family service and when I went forward for communion I suddenly felt at peace

and knew it was all right. I don't know what happened – no noises in my head – but I knew it was all right; I had peace and I still have. I had never been to a communion rail before in my life and at that time I didn't actually take communion but I did take a blessing....

He now sees 9 July 1989 as the date of his conversion.

After going to the communion rail I now found that I wanted to go to church coupled with the response of my daughter being so pleased.

This happened in a Methodist church and he was later baptized and confirmed:

to make public what I had recently come to believe was correct.

◆

◆ Surprisingly few of our respondents described being forced to go to church as youngsters. What effect did it have on John's life and outlook on Christianity? If it is wrong to force children to go to church, what does your church have to be and do in order to attract them?

◆ "I don't believe in religion but it is good for the children." This is a common reaction (especially by men). What is a possible response to this statement?

◆ Our research showed that a number of people, like John, found "going forward to receive a blessing" at the Eucharist to be a very significant step in their spiritual journey. Does your church offer this as a possibility, and is it seen as more than a formality?

Rachel

FINDING THE MESSIAH

It is likely that only a comparatively small number of those of other faiths are coming to the Christian faith in England at present. Of the 511 people who were interviewed in the research project only two or three came within that category. There were a number of others who had shown an interest in Buddhism and other eastern religions but of those who had been brought up in another faith very few had turned to Christianity.

Rachel was brought up as a Jew. She went to synagogue about once a month. Then:

> Jewish teaching stops at 13 then you go to adult class – but I did not go.

She found the Jewish Youth Study Group "interesting" but it gave her a "negative" view of the Christian faith. She went to an ordinary state school but was "not allowed to go to religious study regarding Christianity". As a Jew she studied the Old Testament and found it "old-fashioned in a positive sense" and "fascinating".

Her spiritual search began while she was still in the Youth Study Group:

> When I went to the synagogue it was as if God was not there. Yet when I went on holiday we visited old churches and even there I could feel God's presence.

Rachel had a sudden conversion when she was 33 – five years before we interviewed her. She "needed God, felt helpless". She was facing an operation, and a divorce and felt:

> Topsy-turvy, clinically depressed.

During this period of her life she had a narrow escape:

> While I was driving, a car came round a bend on the same side of the road as myself. It lifted over the top of my car. I don't know how I missed it but neither me nor the car were damaged. It made me aware of the saints and death ... what is after this?

She got in touch with a Roman Catholic priest:

> Made a commitment to go and see him regularly. It was helpful to speak
> to someone who gave counselling for divorce and help in other things.

She was aware of "the negative side of God" as she battled with divorce and depression because:

> He seemed threatening and at times "distant".

She began to read the New Testament and to pray more, and wondered if the parables and miracles were to be interpreted literally. But the element in the Christian faith which she found most appealing was

> The Trinity and the bond of love which holds it together.

She decided to become a Christian. It changed her life and found it had:

> given me strength, serenity, gentleness and made me less critical.

Others too have found her

> a nicer person, more relaxed and happy, less uptight and less self-critical.

It is interesting that someone from a totally non-Christian background found starting to go to church "very easy". She

> felt welcome, comfortable and I wanted to be there. I needed to be there
> for instruction class.

She married her new husband in a Catholic church and began the Rite of Christian Initiation of Adults (RCIA). Probably because of her Jewish background Roman Catholic ideals and academic study were explained to her by a priest in a one to one situation. This was followed by

> a "special service" where adult baptism, confirmation and acceptance
> took place at the same time.

She goes to church once a week and would like to be more involved but is hampered by a new baby.

◆

It is too easy to oversimplify a person's life but there seem to have been several factors which helped Rachel to faith: emotional turmoil; spiritual dissatisfaction; a new understanding of God; encounter with a Christian. This blending of the emotional, spiritual, intellectual and social are very common in the stories which we looked at. Seldom does it appear that only one part of a person's life was being touched. When we help people to faith we need to be aware of all the facets of their life. Too often we concentrate on only one, e.g. the emotional (through counselling), intellectual (through teaching), and social (through joining the church).

◆ We asked people which part of the Christian faith they found particularly appealing. Only Rachel, a Jew, mentioned the Trinity. Does this imply that the doctrine is little taught in our churches or that it is not understood? This revelation of the being of God is one of the most pivotal parts of Christianity. How many can pass it on to others?

Ruth

COMPLETION

I started to feel that my life was incomplete: I had all the material things I needed but something was missing. It was then that I started to go to church again and slowly but surely became aware of God in a way I hadn't before. I began to feel that he was there watching when I needed him and felt more and more comforted by that.

Ruth said that the process of moving from a semi-Christian background to an awareness of God's presence took two years. There were many people in the research who echoed St Augustine's words: "Our hearts are restless till they find their rest in Thee."

Her upbringing was conventional. Brought up in a family which was reasonably positive towards the Christian faith, she went to Sunday School on and off until she was 14. Then:

I felt no need for the church at that time.

Many years passed with little or no contact with the church. She left school at 16, married and had children:

> My children attend a church school and because of that I became more aware and involved in the church.

She was particularly helped by the vicar:

> because he's a compassionate and inspiring person.

However, it was some time before that general interest turned into a conscious awareness of God. Ruth is careful to point out that:

> my sister, whom I am very close to, was suffering from breast cancer. That wasn't the reason why I became a more committed Christian but my concern for my sister dominated much of my life at that time.

Ruth describes her feelings at this time:

> I was excited and eager to be more committed and filled with anxiety about my sister at the same time.

Her view of God was also changing. Before this period she had seen him vaguely as "a spirit". Now he was being seen as

> a friend and comforter and guide.

From going to church occasionally, she now:

> felt a compulsion to go.

This in time led to her asking to begin confirmation preparation

> because I felt I wasn't complete.

Although she would have liked more Bible study and discussion, she enjoyed the preparation groups and her confirmation was

> one of the most moving moments of my life.

She sums up her life now, after the period of change:

> I feel a more complete person.

♦

The sense of "something missing" which Ruth describes is common. It is very difficult for those experiencing this to talk about, because they do not have the language. Respondents in the research spoke about "a gap in my life", "a sense of unease".

♦ This feeling is often used by the Holy Spirit to draw people to God. Sensitive and thoughtful questions may help such people to express their feelings and understand what they are experiencing, e.g. "Do you think, that God may be trying to tell you something?" What are the needs of such people likely to be and how can we serve them?

I have given this woman the name Ruth, because Ruth was the book of the Bible which had meant the most to her.

Martha

YOU SHALL RETURN WITH JOY

When I married at 21 I left the church completely and over the years convinced myself that there was not a God who cared, and I did not really believe in Jesus Christ any more. After an absence from the church of about 30 years, and because of growing unhappiness, I rejoined the Methodist church. Through the past year God has shown me that he does care and has forgiven me for deserting him.

Martha is now 54. She went to church every week until she was 19 and yet appears to have abandoned her faith completely for many years.

Three factors drew her back to God:

A Jehovah's Witness called on me several times at a time when life was beginning to have little meaning for me and I was deeply unhappy. Through her I began to wonder if that was where I had gone so wrong in deserting God. That particular faith (JW) did not appeal to me, so I decided to go to a Methodist Church service (I knew someone who was a keen Methodist whom I admired greatly). The minister offered to come and talk to me. He seemed very caring and suggested that I try several of the local churches to see which one I felt happy in. I did this and found a great deal of warmth from the Christians in one particular church which happened to be the one of the above minister.

Three people were used by God to bring Martha to faith. The Jehovah's Witness ... the Methodist lay person ("whose lifestyle and attitude I admired very much") ... the minister ("sympathetic and caring, but definitely not too pushing, which would have put me off").

The change when it came was sudden:

> I had a particularly unhappy day in March last year. I went to bed early and started to read a book by Catherine Marshall called *Beyond Ourselves*. The book touched me and I realized how selfish, greedy, and bitter I had become. The tears began to pour down my face and I really cried out to God for help. Suddenly, all my mental pain seemed to stop as if I was drugged (but I wasn't). I felt an incredible peace. All I could think was – God has touched me and I can feel it.

At the time she was

> Very unhappy and often so depressed that I wished I could die but didn't have the courage to do anything about it.

She knows that the process is continuing:

> Slowly, since then, I think I am changing. Certainly I have changed inside. I really feel now that Jesus is in me and I am in him. I have since had another similar experience recently and I feel more peace within than I have ever felt in my life before.

Martha gives the impression of having come out of a protective cage and found that

> other people are on the whole much nicer than I used to think they were and so I think it is making me more friendly to them, and in turn happier.

She had begun a course on the pastoral care of the mentally ill with a view to befriending someone who was suffering from mental illness.

She saw these changed relationships with others as being the bedrock of her faith. When we asked her what "being a Christian" meant to her, she said:

> It means loving people. Being free from bitterness, hatred, jealousy, anger – all the negative emotions. Thinking of others and knowing that none of us is any better than each other.

> (Realistically she comments "I am not saying that I have managed to attain all these qualities".)

She describes God as:

> in all the elements of nature. I confess that I do not understand him but I only know that he comes to my aid when I ask him over the basic things, i.e. giving me peace, calm and some confidence (which I did not have before).

It was by no means all straightforward. Martha commented that her husband and sons were either "neutral" or "negative" to the Christian faith, but her faith and life within the church means a very great deal to her.

♦

♦ Martha's faith enabled her to express her personality fully. Her healing had been noticed by others. Her friends had commented that she "had come out of her shell" and "seemed happier". This new Martha was more outgoing, more aware of others, less self-absorbed and self-conscious. The negative emotions which had closed her to others were draining away. How far does your church help and expect a new outlook on life in those who become its members?

♦ Martha had a strong sense of having deserted God. How common is this feeling? How can we help people who feel like this, remembering that we do not want to meet people whom we think we have betrayed, let alone God?

Jeanette

SALVATIONIST SOLDIER

Jeanette is a 16-year-old studying for her A levels. She has been brought up involved in the Salvation Army since she was a baby. A year ago she made a step of further commitment and became a soldier in the Army. In her preparation for this

> they explained exactly what I would be signing my name to, and made sure I was ready for the commitment.

But her spiritual history is not as simple as it might seem. At the age of 12 her world seemed to be falling apart:

> My parents' marriage was breaking up after several years of unhappiness. My dad was beating me up as well.

From then until she was 14 she experienced a gradual turning to God. Another Christian helped her:

> He was there to explain all that I didn't understand, through the good and the bad times. He really understood my difficulties and was caring and sensitive to my needs, which at times were very special due to a situation that I was in at the time. He had a special faith that I didn't have and I wanted.

During this two-year period she describes herself as

> confused and emotional and very scared of what every new day would bring. However, I had a great sense of peace knowing that God was near ... I just gradually realized that God wanted and deserved more than I was giving.

Other things made an impression:

> Going to hear Nikki Cruz in Croydon was a very moving experience and one that I won't forget. God seemed very real and I've never seen so many seekers.

> Reading the books of Joni Eareckson has been very helpful as it has proved that God is real and is always there.

She now feels that before this time she knew that God "was there but wasn't close at all". Now

> he is with me all the time, sharing in everything I do, showing the way he wants me to go.

This means:

> I have a better sense of where my life is going. I'm happier and calmer. I don't worry as much.

♦

When asked when she became a Christian Jeanette replied "9 years ago": i.e. when she was 7 years old. She said this because she was "too young to have a faith before 7 years of age". From her story it could be suggested that she had always been a Christian but that she had come to a deeper realization of God between the ages of 12 and 14. But it is also possible that she became a Christian at the age of 7. Only God knows the answer to that one and it is pointless to speculate.

However, her comment raises the important point:

♦ Can a baby or a young child become a Christian?

Wanda

BAPTIZED BANNER-MAKER

Far more women were statisically the "main factor" in bringing their partners to faith than vice versa (22 per cent compared to 5 per cent). Wanda is one of the minority. She was 21 and newly married:

> My husband was most important because I knew that while I did not go to church he would not go. I never stopped him from going, but knew he really wanted to go but would not without me. We had tried lots of churches while we had been courting but none appealed to me. Then, one day, I decided I wanted to learn and know more about God, so I took action. Just before the time I started going to church (my husband never pushed me) but I know now that he asked God for his help in making me want to go to church.

> When I was married I thought more about Christ because of my husband.

Things started to develop when she was watching TV:

> I had been thinking of the church a little beforehand with being newly married and my husband being a Christian, but one night I went along to my friend's house as usual and when I got there *Songs of Praise* was on the television. The *Songs of Praise* was showing a baptism. My friend asked me if I had ever thought about being baptized and I said "Yes – since I've been married" but did not know how to approach anyone to do with the church. At this time she said if I really wanted she would come to see the minister with me and ask what had to be done for me to be baptized. That night I went along to the minister's house with my friend and as she could not see me then we made a date to have a chat. It just went from there. My husband was not in any church at the time and was thrilled when I told him the news.

Wanda was one of the 20 per cent of our respondents who had had no Christian background. She was not baptized as a baby and had no contact with church apart from a short spell in the Guides.

> We had to go to church once a month and at this time I found church uninteresting. Only went because I had to.

She never read the Bible or any other Christian book, never saw a Christian film and her schools did not help her towards Christ.

However, and it is important, she did pray:

> I did not really think of God, only when I prayed at night; then I thought of him as someone who would help in time of need.

Despite her very limited experience of church she found it "quite easy" to start to go to the local Methodist church with her presumably excited and thankful husband.

> I want to learn about Christ and to meet and mix with Christians. Other social outings just happen now on days I do not go to church.

Her view of God has deepened and become more personal. Instead of God being someone to help her in her "time of need",

> God is wonderful, kind, loving, and the person who knows me best. He is with me all the time and makes a warm feeling in my stomach.

The minister prepared her for baptism on a one-to-one basis:

> With never having a Christian upbringing I did not know a lot. The lady who I went to learnt me how to understand things about the faith and gave me confidence.

The baptism service was "very worthwhile".

> It made me feel good inside that I had told everyone how I felt about becoming a Christian.

She is now involved in

> a banner group once every week, and every other week after the banner group we have a Bible study.

◆

♦ Wanda says that long before she had anything to do with the church, she prayed "every day". It is a remarkable fact that far more people pray than go to any church or profess any faith openly. For the Christian church it is both a challenge and an opportunity. Can we say "Perhaps we can share together about prayer so that we can learn together about God?"

♦ Perhaps a "School of Prayer" could be a major evangelistic event if it was seen as something for everyone and not just for churchgoers.

Jack

POWER EVANGELISM

Jack was 55 when it all happened to him:

Shortly after we had moved to X my wife joined the local Anglican church. Within a short period of time I noticed there was something different about her when she returned home from the morning service. I can best describe it as a warm glow or radiance. She was always anxious to tell me about the wonderful preaching and fellowship. One Sunday I decided to see what was going on. The peace, love and power was evident from that very first visit and my Christian commitment has gone from strength to strength since that time.

He was particularly struck by

the directness, truth and love in our vicar's sermons. I always found his words so challenging; sometimes the truth was often disturbing. Our vicar posed many questions in my lifestyle, so I became a regular churchgoer to hear those challenging sermons in the hope that I would find some of the answers to these questions.

As Jack hints, there were things in his life which he felt guilty about, but the overwhelming feeling at this time was

excitement and eagerness in discovering the new direction in my life and the feeling of joy at Christian meetings.

A short time afterwards, Jack and his wife went to a "Praise and Worship" evening in the nearby town:

> At the end of the service a time of ministry was always available for people with various problems. On this particular evening my wife went forward for a back problem. I also moved forward (not sure why). When I went to the front somebody started praying for me to be filled with the Holy Spirit. At that moment I felt my arms moving upwards but not under my own control. Then I felt a great warmth flowing through my body and I began shaking violently for some minutes – I was aware of the person praying for more power and I felt as though I was going to explode. From that day onwards my life has changed completely.

After this happened Jack

> had a great thirst to read and understand the Bible, and an eagerness to attend as many Christian meetings as possible to hear different speakers preaching the Word of God.

Not surprisingly, he found it "very easy" to start going to church regularly because

> I had a real thirst to find the answers to all the questions that were being brought to the surface in my life each time I attended church.

Until this time in his life Jack had had a humdrum spiritual career. He "drifted away from Sunday School when I joined the local youth and cycling club". He was also a scout but

> I felt that the lack of commitment from the group leaders probably moved me away from Christianity.

He became a very occasional churchgoer, sometimes turning up at Christmas or Easter. It was what he describes as "a lukewarm approach". At this time he thought of God as

> a mysterious presence somewhere out in the universe who created all things.

After his sudden change of outlook he still saw God as "the Creator of all things", but also someone

> who I can now have a Father relationship with because he gave his Son Jesus for my sins on the cross, thus sending the Holy Spirit as mediator.

Following the change in his life he felt he needed to be baptized and confirmed (although he had been baptized as a child):

> I felt I had reached the stage in my Christian life when it was right to declare my faith in public ... I hoped that by my public declaration I would encourage others to do the same.

◆

About 16 per cent of the people who were interviewed spoke about some "charismatic" happening – usually healing or, as in Jack's case, being "filled with the Spirit". Often it was associated with the laying on of hands with prayer (less frequently with anointing).

> ◆ Should our churches offer this ministry to both churchgoers and non-churchgoers – "always available for people with problems"?

Jack was typical:

> ◆ men more often than women spoke of the influence that preaching had had in their spiritual growth

> ◆ older people are more likely to have a "sudden" conversion experience

> ◆ men were far more likely to say that their wives had been the main factor in bringing them to God than vice versa.

> ◆ Some of these findings are puzzling. Is there anything we can learn from them?

Joanna

RANSOMED, HEALED, RESTORED, FORGIVEN

Most of the people who had no church background at all came from homes which were indifferent to the Christian faith. Joanna came from one which was actively antagonistic, yet as a girl there was a yearning:

> I would try to watch films about Jesus because I wanted to know more about him. My family didn't love me and I got comfort through watching those films, but I had to be careful that my parents did not find out. When I watched those films I got a warm glow inside me. I wanted to know more but I didn't know who to ask. There were so many questions that I wanted answers to. I wanted to be loved so much by Jesus but my family condemned him. I used to watch the films secretly.

Joanna had no experience of church at all during her childhood. She grew up, married, had two children, divorced. At the age of 36

> I had just lost my two children to my father and I was afraid of the future. I had also come out of a treatment centre (I was an alcoholic and an addict). I had nowhere to live. But through prayer I lived with a family and then I got a bedsit.

However, despite this and an involvement with the occult, her childhood longing for Jesus was still there:

> I felt warm inside when Jesus was mentioned. The world looked different to me and slowly I began to pray and my prayers were answered.

At about this time she had an experience of God:

> I was on the common and the wind was gently blowing. I was all alone with just the cattle and horses. Suddenly I felt a warm feeling come over me. I distinctly heard my name. I looked round. No one was there. Again I heard my name. Before I knew what happened I was down on my knees praying. I felt that everything was going to be OK. When

people saw me they said that my face was shining. I felt strong and alive. I *know* that, that day, God had spoken to me. From that day on, I have followed Christ.

Somehow, we are not told how, she got in contact with her local Anglican church and met the vicar:

He talked to me and prayed with me. He helped me to get to the Healing Centre. He talked to me about God in simple words that I could understand. He gave me strength when I felt too weak to carry on.

It was the Healing Centre that Joanna now sees as being the main factor that brought her to God:

I had been involved with the occult for a long time. I went to a Healing Centre because I wanted to be free from Satan. I spent a week there and I could feel the fight going on between Jesus and Satan. The people there all prayed with me and one day I was set free. I screamed out the name "Jesus" and the chains were broken. I can now speak in tongues and I get visions. My life since I have been a Christian has changed completely. Without the Healing Centre I would be dead now. There is power in prayer. Now I belong to God and *nothing* can take me away.

It is not surprising that when we asked Joanna what particularly appealed to her about the Christian message she mentioned the parable of the lost sheep.

Joanna began to go to church with a friend. It was difficult, not because of the liturgy and culture but because:

I felt dirty and I shouldn't be there because I felt unworthy. It was a house of God and I felt he did not want me.

Now, two years after first becoming part of the congregation:

... it is alive with hope and peace. The people are my family, with God at the head.

With Joanna's past history in mind it is good to hear her testimony:

Jesus has forgiven all my sins and I need not walk in fear again. Everything has a purpose in God's plan. Through God I will live for ever. God is my Father and my friend. If I have problems I take them to the Lord in prayer. He is *always* with me. I am not alone any more. He loves me.

Her previous view of God was very different:

> He was a punishing God. He was a judge and very stern. He would send me to hell when I died. He would turn his back on me and tell me that I was not worthy. He didn't want me.

This total change in Joanna did not go unnoticed. She recalls some of the comments that were made to her:

> "You have light in your eyes"
> "You don't worry like you used to"
> "You love God because your voice is gentle when you talk about him"
> "You laugh a lot more now"

A year after her first contact with the church she was baptized and confirmed:

> I wanted people to know that through God I had changed and that there is always hope.

At the service she gave her testimony:

> People came up to me and wanted to know if Jesus could love them. They wanted to know more about him. I made a lot of Christians through my talk and I was declaring God's love.

Joanna's story is not yet finished. Shortly before she filled in her questionnaire:

> I had been on crutches for a long time. I had problems with my knee. I went to the healing service and had my knee prayed for. That night as I went to bed I felt my knee get warm. My friend felt my knee and she could feel it. I felt my leg getting stronger and I put my crutches to one side. I felt something pulling me forward and I started walking. I felt no pain and I was not limping. To this day I have had no trouble with the knee.

♦

Joanna's story is one of the most extraordinary that we received. There are many points for learning and discussion which could come from it, not least the transparent depth of her present faith and the way in which she has received healing of body, mind and spirit.

However, there are times, after hearing a story like Joanna's, when we need simply to worship and thank the God who redeems.

Joan

PARENTAL INFLUENCE?

Joan was 65 when she reaffirmed her childhood faith. When asked about the difference that this made in her life Joan said:

> I have a lot more friends in church and a commitment to the church. I've become an elder and play the organ so I'm much busier. I feel happier, I feel I'm doing the right thing ... the guilt has gone. I'm more tolerant.

When someone becomes a Christian there are social changes as well as spiritual ones. Before Joan had reaffirmed her faith she had only gone to church two or three times a year. Now she goes "more than once a week". Around the time of her recommitment she retired from teaching, so she has more time, but as she says, "it's important to be active in your faith". Church and its activities play a major part in her life and she is now an elder of her URC church.

Joan's parents were from different denominations – her mother was Methodist, her father Unitarian – and they had been keen that she should go to Sunday School. She went "every week". Clearly they had been influential for her

> parents were very kind and practised what they preached – not so strong on church attendance.

Sunday School was no chore for Joan – she "always looked forward to going". Although she did not go to a church school quite a lot of emphasis was given to religion in her schools. Her secondary school in particular made her more thoughtful about the faith and her time in Guides clearly reinforced this. She also read the Bible "several times a week".

Joan is typical of many older respondents. She was encouraged in Christian belief at home, this was reinforced at school and Sunday School. She had enjoyed her faith:

> The vicar at the first Anglican church I went to impressed me. When I first went as a girl it was because the organist invited me to learn the organ after going to the service. I'm very interested in music.

But she lacked a vital ingredient: her parents did not set her an example of churchgoing. Nothing made her a disciple. Despite all the favourable signs Joan ceased going to church in her mid-teens. She says now that she remained a Christian and prayed regularly during the forty or so years between her teenage years and the time when things began to change. But apart from a very occasional visit, she ceased to be a churchgoer.

Joan is typical of so many older people. They have a good grounding in the Christian faith but they grow out of it as they become older. They still have their faith but it largely lies dormant apart from prayer.

Joan expected her children to follow her own path:

> I sent my own children to church because I was friendly with the teacher who ran the Sunday School there and my children were friends with her girl.

Even at that point she "felt that it was not fair to send them and not go myself", but she did nothing about it for many years. It was not until the *wedding* of her daughter when Joan was 65 that this sense of unease translated into action. From time to time during those years the idea of getting herself right with God and joining a church must have surfaced, but the right opportunity never occurred. There must be many Joans who think wistfully from time to time of joining a church but never have the courage to make the step. They have a good knowledge of the faith, they pray, they are keen for their family to have connections with the church but never actually make it. Her experience at the wedding made all the difference:

> I thought everyone was so helpful and nice and I didn't want to use the church – I wanted to give something back.

The guilt she had felt when she sent the children to Sunday School and did not do anything about it herself came back – and this time she acted. At first:

> I was shy, but gradually I lost my inhibitions.

A little while later she was asked if she would become a member at the ceremony of reaffirmation:

> made me more committed – it's very important to be committed.

The sense of faith she had had as a child was reawakened. The gap of forty years was behind her.

♦

One wonders whether Joan's parents' lack of church attendance was because of the different denominations – often families duck a difficult issue by evading church altogether. We need to remember that Joan's childhood would have been in the 1920s and 1930s when changing churches was much less common than today and the ecumenical acceptance by Christians of each other was only in its infancy.

> ♦ How can we help people to talk through and make decisions about such matters when they come from different church traditions?

It is noticeable that Joan followed her parents' example – sending her children to Sunday School but not going herself.

Margaret

DEEPER AND DEEPER INTO CHRIST

Margaret is in her early forties, owner of a shop, living in a pleasant neighbourhood. She is a member of a House church which meets nearby.

She was brought up as an Anglican. Her parents did not go to church but she was encouraged to go to Sunday School. She liked going and went regularly until she was 12. Then she stopped, like so many. However, her twelve months in a Church of England primary school "had lasting effects". Very few of our respondents were so strongly favourable about their school experience.

But Margaret did come back to church at 16 and was confirmed:

> I didn't understand confirmation at all; it didn't make any difference to me. But, looking back, I think the making of promises must have made some difference in a spiritual sense.

But this period of churchgoing only lasted a year or so. Her parents moved. She lived in lodgings and spent weekends in their new home where she knew no one:

> parents weren't involved with church so I didn't go either.

When she married, her husband was linked with a URC church and she met the minister there. Later she came to regard the minister as the most important factor in her becoming a Christian. Her husband's job moved them abroad for a time but they still kept in touch with him. On returning to the same area some years later, churchgoing was spasmodic. They had their children baptized in his church and they went a few times a year, but it was an arm's length relationship with God and with the church.

Then the local Christian Fellowship carried out a survey and invited her to church. She was 41. Life was

> stressful, due to our own business responsibilities ... crowded with activities and work.
>
> I went to church on Sunday and was immediately overwhelmed by the love and presence of the Holy Spirit. I cried, but didn't understand. I was handed a booklet entitled *What's the Point?* I then committed my life to Christ. The deeper commitment came after an ongoing process at the time of my baptism – three months later.
>
> I was hooked from making my initial commitment to Jesus. I couldn't wait for Sunday to come round to be with the other Christians.

Margaret shows well the ladder of events which so often is present when someone makes a commitment to Christ. She herself says that she never knew a time when she was not a Christian and that the commitment in the House church was a recommitment, just as her baptism was a rebaptism. Her early interest in the Christian faith, the force which drew her to confirmation at 17, the friendship with the URC minister, the occasional churchgoing all played their part, but it was the incident in the House church which made it all come together, and that led to an even "deeper commitment" at her baptism.

◆

The different stages in her commitment show vividly in Margaret's story. For many people it is like peeling an onion – they make a commitment of themselves to Christ ... then the Holy Spirit reveals more which needs to be committed and that leads to a deeper commitment ... then the Holy Spirit reveals more....

Her story also shows the need for a commitment to Christ at different stages in our life. The offering we bring to Christ as a child is different from that which we can bring as an adult, but in its way is just as important.

> ◆ How can we help people to see that it is a continual commitment of our lives to Christ which is important; not just a one-off event which recedes into the past?

Tessa

NOT ASHAMED

Research shows that while congregations bring new people into the church, it is the minister who keeps them there. Usually this is done, not by preaching or the way they take services, but by friendliness and counsel.

Tessa, now in her fifties, gives her assessment of the ministers she has met. Her own minister

> cared about individuals and not all of them do. To be honest there are only four of them I have met who I can relate to – one when I was 8, then 32, then 47, then 52.

Tessa says that she gradually became a Christian between the ages of 21 and 54. However, the period that was particularly significant was when she was surrounded by a series of desperate situations:

> My children were near starvation; we were homeless. My son developed a heart condition. My mother became an alcoholic and took numerous attempts at suicide.

(Tessa gives no further details of her situation at this time but records that she is separated from her husband.)

It was at this point that the minister of the church she was loosely attached to played a crucial role:

> The vicar at that time gave me reason to believe in God's love and didn't make me feel inadequate.

> He also gave my son a reason to live, I still don't know how. When he was 11 years he wanted to die because he said "a third of the world is starving, a third of the world is fighting (Vietnam) – and the worst is the other third doesn't care". Every time the hospital got his heart back to normal it [the heart problem] would start again. The reverend went into the theatre with him and when I went to see him my son said "I'm going to get better now, Mum." I still to this day don't know what was said and I promised I wouldn't ask.

Tessa hints many times at her own feelings of self-worth. She went to Sunday School until she was 11 but stopped

> because I didn't feel good enough to go into church.

At the traumatic period of her life she describes her state of mind as being "not good enough", and so she turned to the vicar because he did not make her feel "inadequate". She enjoyed the group meetings in preparation for her confirmation

> because at each lesson we were all allowed our say and no one laughed.

The acceptance by the minister and by the church was of enormous significance to her. She found it "quite easy" to start going

> because she was welcomed.

She decided to be confirmed

> because I felt loved and forgiven.

It was this all-welcoming grace of God which most attracted her to the

> loving, forgiving Father of the world.

It was a great time for her and at her confirmation she was able to say

> I was not ashamed to declare I was a Christian to anyone.

One feels that for Tessa that was victory indeed.

♦

Tessa is someone who is very unsure of herself, easily frightened and uneasy in a group. Her journey to full commitment took no less than 33 years. The unconditional love of God in Christ she saw written in human lives through the minister and the congregation were the Bible coming alive for her. Jesus was very gentle with the "bruised reed" and the "little ones" and very stern with those who hurt them. He gave power to the hesitant, guidance to the lost, acceptance to the despised. He still touches the "leper" through his people.

> ♦ Who are the "lepers" in your community and how can we touch them with the hand of Christ?

Sandra

PASTORAL CARE

Sandra lists the most important elements in her gradual journey to faith (over a period of seven years):

- ♦ my marriage
- ♦ our house move
- ♦ diagnosis of infertility
- ♦ birth of my daughter and later my confirmation in the Anglican church.

Sandra's childhood was difficult. She was brought up as a Methodist and regularly went to Sunday School. However,

> after some personal experiences my father became an atheist, my mother was basically a humanist though brought up a Methodist.

There were family difficulties and Sandra was sent off to live with an aunt and uncle, who were her godparents:

> they steered me into the church when I lived with them. At about 12 or 13 I moved back with my parents and slowly my attendance tailed off.

However, her secondary school (which was not a church one) put "quite a lot" of emphasis on the Christian faith and she read the Bible from time to time although no longer going to church. There were other influences:

> I remember going to see *Godspell* in London when I had stopped going to Sunday School. It was marvellous and exhilarating, and I remember crying with shame and distress at the crucifixion, but it certainly re-awakened my beliefs and I bought the record of the show and listened to it endlessly and I looked up the verses in the Bible that they had taken excerpts from.

> I also remember watching some of the Lent programmes which were broadcast from Jerusalem and being inspired by the film of the actual places mentioned in the Bible. It brought home the history and reality of it.

Apart from that, and a reasonably regular prayer life, Sandra had no contact with the Christian church until she married:

> My husband came from a very committed Christian family with a history of family members working in a cathedral, so he tended to steer me into the Anglican church. However, when we lived in X, the local church was high C of E and vicar was not keen that I attended because I wouldn't change denomination, but when we moved we oscillated between the United Reformed and the C of E until one member of the C of E congregation asked why we went to both, since she felt we belonged to the Anglican church. I was apprehensive that the vicar would put pressure on me to become an Anglican but he never did but he gradually involved me in various church activities, and he also helped me in counselling through my infertility problems, so eventually after my daughter was born and christened I asked the rector to include me in confirmation classes as I now felt it was the right time for it.

Looking back, Sandra sees the time when she became pregnant as the time when she began to give herself more to God:

> I thought I would never have any children and when after several years, drug treatment worked and our daughters were born, I felt so blessed and so thankful that my prayers had been answered that I needed to go and constantly give thanks for the pure joy that they gave us.

Nevertheless the pregnancy and time after the birth did not go smoothly:

> I had injured my knee while pregnant and had spent the whole time in plaster up to my hip, in and out of hospital and I was finding life very difficult, my daughter was being child-minded out for the first time ever and she was very distressed. The church friends were very supportive and helpful, running about for me, taking me to physiotherapy, etc.

The help of the church meant a great deal to Sandra and the vicar had helped her through the initial disappointments about infertility, the joy of her pregnancy and the difficulties caused by her injury:

> He never put pressure on me to attend church meetings, merely asked me in passing if I would care to join in. He never pressured me to convert to the Anglican [church], but by his patience and tolerance I was drawn further into the faith, because I wanted to rather than because I felt obliged to.

This excellent pastoral care paid off and, despite Sandra describing herself as "extremely tense and anxious" during this time she finally became a committed Christian. She showed this by being confirmed "because I felt that it was right to do so".

Sandra's story shows the importance of good pastoral care over a long period. And during most of that time she was not even a member of the denomination concerned. Both the counselling which the minister gave her and the practical help given by members of the congregation were significant. It is not difficult to see the cost to the church in terms of the time and energy it took from the people who were caring for Sandra.

♦ Do we sometimes ignore the evangelistic potential of care in the name of Christ in favour of something which appears to be quicker and "more spiritual"?

Joy

THE BIBLE AND BILLY GRAHAM

Joy was 28 when her childhood interest in the Christian faith began to re-awaken:

About six months before I was born again I began to take an interest in the Bible. I only had a children's Bible but I enjoyed reading it because I could understand it. I read it from the beginning right to the end. It was only stories about characters and events, but it was when I began to read the life of Jesus and the letters of the apostles that I began to question. The beatitudes were written so that a child could understand them and some of the exhortations of the apostles were written in such a way too. These began to have an impact on how I thought about my own life and they went deep into my spirit. At 28 I read a child's Bible and I came into the Kingdom of God like a child.

A little later

I was moved by the Holy Spirit to attend a Billy Graham live-link night at a local church. I say I was moved by the Holy Spirit because there was no human that was involved other than myself. I thought I was a Christian, I did not know the meaning of the word evangelism and I had no idea who Billy Graham was. I heard about him on the radio, saw a poster about him and then on my way home from work one day saw the signposts to the event. I followed them to the church, went in to see what was going on, somehow feeling that if I could just enter the building I might get right with God. At the altar call I was almost wrenched from my seat by the Holy Spirit and was subsequently born again.

While she had some sense of guilt about one particular matter, in general she felt good about life:

I was more settled in my mind as well as in my surroundings than I had been since I was a teenager leaving home. I was more confident in myself than I had ever been and life ahead looked pretty good.

Joy had been brought up in a nominally C of E home and gone fairly frequently to Sunday School. Indeed she began to play a leader's part:

I used to take 3-4 year-olds at Sunday School and I had to prepare them for that from printed matter. I was about 12 years old, but I was more interested in the children than what I was teaching them.

Nevertheless her faith meant much to her at this time:

I used to have an old hymn-book at home and liked to sing the hymns in my bedroom. I used to sing Sunday School hymns a lot from my head all day in the week.

I absolutely loved to watch films on TV from the Bible and I remember a lot of them that were shown at Easter, like *Jesus of Nazareth*.

Sadly, this early enthusiasm waned:

I was conscious that it was not fashionable to my age group and those I sought favour from out of my peers would scoff at my "religion".

She left school at 16, stayed single and started her own business. Life carried on as normal until the time when she was drawn to the children's Bible.

The Bible reading and the experience at the Billy Graham live-link made a great difference to her life:

Before I was a Christian my life was based on fear and works – trying hard to be the right person so that I would be loved. Now I have love without deserving it and the less I try of everything the more I achieve of Christ.

The comments of others on this change has varied:

> Non-Christian friends have commented that I am boring, need to let my hair down and have more fun. Christian friends have commented that I am now more open and expressive and able to look people in the eye and hold my head up.

♦

Much comment was made when this research was first published that there were few examples of people being brought to Christ by evangelistic events (4 per cent said it was the main factor in bringing them to faith and 13 per cent said it was a supporting, but not the main, factor). Joy is an example of one of the latter group. She now feels that it was her encounter with the Bible which was the most important thing that happened and that the Billy Graham live-link continued the work which the Bible had begun. It is important to recognize that for some, like Joy, the event may be the culmination of a process. For others it may be the beginning of a new interest in the faith without any commitment.

Jean

RESTORATION

Jean is typical of many. She was part of a church until her teens but stopped going quite suddenly. After eighteen years, when she was 34 she began to go again. During these eighteen years she did not go to church at all and describes her faith as "apathetic".

She lists her reasons for leaving church at 16:

- ♦ I questioned my beliefs
- ♦ peer pressure
- ♦ I was working for exams.

> My parents did not go to church – that must have a bearing on it. They had a newsagents, so they couldn't go on Sundays as they were working.

The list is a familiar one:

- ◆ intellectual questioning
- ◆ going with the crowd
- ◆ work pressure
- ◆ little support from the family.

Yet Jean had been involved with her Anglican church for sixteen years, been confirmed and had a supportive secondary school. But she never read her Bible privately. The book she remembers with affection is *Pilgrim's Progress*.

Jean did not have a sudden conversion. It was a gradual process which began with a spiritual search because...

> I had a miscarriage – during the grieving process I realized something was missing in my life.

The search was thorough:

> We went to three churches in the area and liked the worship best at the one we go to now – also the welcome we received there had quite a big influence.

She and her solicitor husband ended up going to the Baptist church, where she met a group of friends:

> They had something that I hadn't got and that I would like.

She describes restarting church as "quite difficult":

> Even though I had been to Sunday School it was a step into the unknown. Thinking back I felt I was being led to church – almost as though it was out of my control.

There were stereotypes which had to be overcome:

> I thought that it would be old-fashioned and I thought Christians were very *serious* people.

> I thought Christians never did anything wrong – that they were perfect.

She was pleasantly surprised and made two important discoveries:

- ◆ The church *has* got humour
- ◆ The church can be as old-fashioned or as modern as the people make it.

As Jean said, "I returned to a much deeper faith than I had when I was a child." At first (typically for someone going through depression):

> I found it quite difficult to believe that your sins could be forgiven – that you could wipe the slate clean and begin again.

Five years later she was baptized:

> it was the best thing that I'd ever done in my life – it felt so right.

♦

> ♦ Is your church working hard enough to counter the difficulties experienced by your young people, especially as they go through transition points: moving home ... experiencing the divorce of their parents ... beginning work ... going to a new place?

Overall 61 per cent said that "Christian friends" (plural) were a significant factor in their becoming a Christian. Only 14 per cent mentioned that a "Christian friend" (single) was important. It seems that the communal life or "fellowship" of a group of Christians who care for each other is extremely attractive.

> ♦ Did the group that Jean became part of think that they were anything very special.

> ♦ Does your group of friends think they're special?

Like many people who have absented themselves from the Christian church for many years and then return at a very emotional time in their life, Jean wanted to mark this new beginning. Baptism was the rite which seemed most appropriate to her in the setting of a Baptist church. Churches which baptize infants need to think very carefully about providing a rite which is psychologically satisfying to mark a return to faith (which can often *feel* – and perhaps is – a new creation).

Pete

NO INTEREST WHATSOEVER

Pete told us of his attitude to the Christian faith ten years before. He underlined it heavily "No interest whatsoever".

This was certainly true of his adult life until he was 51, but as a child, although his family had no time for the Christian faith, he had been taken by a neighbour to the Sunday School at the Methodist church nearby for a number of years. Then

> I became a teenager – lost interest. Friends went to the cinema on Sunday afternoon.

For a short period when he was 15 he was gripped by the Bible:

> I had a period when I read the Bible every day over three months – I really was interested in it. Then it just faded – I wasn't encouraged. The RE teacher and I didn't "click" because he didn't like you to argue with him: you just had to accept what he said.

Shortly afterwards he left school and his long period of "no interest" began. Then, when he was 43, his brother suddenly died of a heart attack:

> I started to go to church. I thought quite a lot of the preacher – but he left and a new guy came. I felt the church was going downhill – I stopped going.

Yet again Pete found himself outside the life of the church, until one Sunday

> in the summer, about 6.30 a.m. I jumped out of bed and went to church at 8 a.m. There was no one there – so I came home dejected and quite annoyed (it was advertised as 8 a.m. Morning Service on the noticeboard).

He was conscious that nothing in particular had triggered this action:

> I was employed, not under any stress – just my normal self. I just woke up with the desire to pray ... I hadn't thought about God or anything the night before.

After a time he summoned up courage again:

> Later in the summer I decided to go again, this time at 10 a.m. The lay
> minister introduced the new preacher – it was the man who had been
> friendly eight years before. I felt that I had made the right decision.

Pete describes this Methodist minister:

> He had time – you can speak to him. He does not fob you off and he
> doesn't preach at you. He's been through the mill a bit himself. He
> became a Christian in the RAF in the Middle East. You can relate to
> someone who has had a bit of a wild life before becoming a Christian.
> Sometimes I wonder when those "schoolboy" Christians preach and tell
> you that life should be rosy. They've never known what it's like to have
> a hard time, so how can they know what it's like for those who have....

Clearly things have changed since the new minster came:

> ...he has altered the structure of the services. I enjoy the "handclapping"
> and seeing teenagers getting involved – not that I do it myself: I'm a bit
> reserved, but it's really uplifting to see them.

When we asked Pete about his understanding of God he said:

> I fall out with him sometimes.

> I don't think we question what happens in our religious lives enough. A
> few weeks ago I was very upset. A Christian lady in the church was dying
> of cancer. Her husband was a Christian too. She wanted to die before
> him – but he died suddenly in his sleep. She was left alone, so she threw
> herself into the river and drowned.

> You profess to believe that God is your friend – but why does he let things
> happen? We should be asking questions: God wants us to ask questions.

Pete started going to church weekly, though he is not able to go as much as he
would like because his wife is not a Christian.

> However, I joined the Bible Study classes which I've been doing ever
> since.

Each morning he reads the Bible:

> I wouldn't have a faith without it – it sets you up for the day.

He also

> gets involved in looking after the church garden and hedges, and the cleaning team which involves you more with people.

His new faith has made a difference to him:

> I think it has quietened me a bit inasmuch as I was quite an explosive person.

For Pete, giving his testimony in church was very significant:

> I felt I needed to ... I wanted to ... it was long overdue. I stood up and declared my love for Jesus Christ. Two of us gave a testimony that night in the service. The other bloke had been a alcoholic and all sorts.

> It blessed me – I don't know if it blessed anyone else.

♦

Very few of the people who were interviewed mentioned any religious questions and uncertainties (apart from a few problems about the Bible). The major issues, such as the problem of suffering which Pete raises, were mentioned in only a few cases, even though we specifically asked a question about it.

> ♦ Does this mean that people who have fairly recently come to faith are not yet ready to face these major topics? Or does it mean that they are happy with the answers they have been given? Or what?

> ♦ Clearly at some point in the Christian life the major theological and ethical questions have to be faced. What is the best point to introduce them and what is the best way to do so?

Kevin

TO WHOM MUCH IS FORGIVEN ...

When he was 28, what he described as a gradual conversion began in Kevin. It lasted about a year

> although my wife led me to Christ, and my pastor and church influenced me accepting Christ, the Bible alone gives me the confirmation of any of the Lord's declarations.

He had come from a "no religion" home and had never been to church. He went to the Boy's Brigade for a while which

> had no effect towards Christianity but gave good moral attitude

but never went on church parade.
　Early in his life he had been impressed by Christianity:

> I remember being totally moved when watching *Godspell* at the Opera House in Manchester. Reduced to tears by the injustice that took place in the life of Jesus ... feeling elated at the life of Jesus in *Jesus of Nazareth*.

He left school at 18 and seems to have experimented with most things:

> Hanuman, Buddhist, Taoist, humanist – in all love was the keyword
>
> God was all in all, everything – all the time at all times.

He joined a woman who showed him something of the Christian path:

> living wrongly in God's eyes – not married, living with the lady who is now my wife.

He says that "repentance" was the thing which he needed most:

> Lots of wrongs (the Lord has commanded through conviction and prayer) made right

smoking being physically admonished from my life

giving up cocaine and cannabis

various other narcotic and hallucinogenic drugs giving up the way to pay for these habits

I had just fathered a baby boy.

Initially, he and his partner went to a Pentecostal church. He found joining the church "quite easy":

family commitments – work commitments were the only initial block.

However, he found that it did not meet all their needs and so joined a Baptist church because they "needed to grow". The pastor of this church had a considerable influence:

through the Holy Spirit he answered our needs, posed examining questions and generally cared for our welfare.

Becoming a Christian for him was life-transforming:

I have been given a sense of self-awareness by Jesus, never ascertained by any other means. I feel secure in understanding Jesus' wants of me.

Not surprisingly

my family (parents, brothers, etc.) have noticed my giving up of bad habits and attitudes.

And he received what seemed to be good-natured teasing at work:

Ask Moses and he will sort it out!

He married the woman he had been living with and saw that and his baptism, which came three months later, as a testimony. He remarks of his baptism service:

it helped others to understand just how Jesus is so important to us all.

He is still not satisfied:

I feel my personal convictions conflict with my life in general. I wish to give everything to our Lord.

♦

Kevin does not set out in detail his life before his conversion but paying for his addictions clearly led him into crime. It was very noticeable in the research that those who had had a very dramatic turn around in lifestyle on finding God were most prepared to give their all to him afterwards. They were not being given a wash and brush-up but a new heart, and Kevin's final remark indicates this.

♦ How can we best serve those people who may not be satisfied by what they regard as the milk and water of life of some of our churches?

Marcia

FROM SECULARISM TO FAITH

"Marcia" is a 28-year-old civil servant, now attending an Anglican church. Her parents had little time for the Christian faith. They were not actively hostile, but they never discussed it. Marcia was never encouraged to go to Sunday School or church as a youngster and never did so, neither did she go to a church school. She describes the religion she learnt about at primary school as having "little or no effect". Her response to her secondary schooling was a little more positive as she remembers that performing *Joseph and the Amazing Technicolor Dreamcoat* had been a help.

Apart from being baptized as a baby and reading the Bible a few times with her grandmother as a small child, she had no direct contact with a group of Christians until she was an adult.

There are many Marcias around today. With no Christian background, no attendance at church or Sunday School, and a largely secular schooling, only the influence of her grandmother (and her prayers?) gave her any understanding of the faith. Her story is particularly important, because it describes the journey to faith of someone with virtually no church background. About one in five of the respondents in the research came into this category – which is good news, for if we were only bringing to God those who had had a Christian background, it would not bode well for our evangelism.

It has been estimated that over 50 per cent of the population come into this category. They are members of no Christian church or any other faith. However, they are not atheists. Marcia says of this period:

I would have said that I believed in God but would have found it difficult to explain any more than that.

So any evangelism which assumes unbelief in God is bound not to be listened to, because the hearers *do* believe. It may seem a very inadequate view of God (see Marcia's beautiful description of her present view of God below), but it is not atheism.

Marcia's journey to faith began when she was 25. Nothing especially good or bad was happening to her. She describes herself as having been happy – another reminder that we can become Christians when we are not going through some great need.

Then she met and talked to some friends who were Christians ... at first informally, then through joining a group. Marcia was helped primarily through:

Discussions, sharing experiences, and together questioning the Christian faith with friends – mainly during our "Exploring Faith" course.

She then started going to church. When we asked her why, she said:

Because I enjoyed it! My going to church helped to strengthen my faith, which led to me being confirmed (at age of 27), and I now get a lot from the communion service.

Marcia was going to church for virtually the first time in her life. And she described it as "quite easy". Christians often suppose that it is a terrible obstacle course which only the bravest can tackle. While we found that those from a non-Christian background, like Marcia, found it more difficult to start going to church, many of them did not find it particularly hard – 68 per cent described it as "quite easy" or "very easy". This remarkable finding is almost certainly due to the fact that the majority of them were first involved in the Christian faith through their friends – who would presumably take them along to church, introduce them to people, show them the way through the service, and generally look after them.

For these people, like many others, one step in their journey to Christ is the invitation, "Would you like to come along to church with me?" Christians often avoid what seems a rather unheroic question, because it appears to talk more about church than about Christ. But at some point in many people's spiritual journey it is the key question. The response of Marcia ("I enjoyed it!"), and many like her who encounter church for the first time, also suggests that Christians do not need to be apologetic about their church. It may, in your opinion, need improving, but for those coming for the first time it can be a place of warmth and welcome.

While it was friends who first brought Marcia to church, it was the minister who helped her in many ways after that:

> My own parish vicar – I very much respect his beliefs and views and the way in which he carries out his "spiritual duties".

Marcia had also found the whole church environment had been helpful, particularly the Eucharist:

> Church activities provide a stable foundation on which one's faith can grow strong enough to support during times of questioning or doubt. Holy Communion itself offers chance for spiritual renewal ... also gives a great sense of community and belonging, and an opportunity for caring.

Marcia speaks here and elsewhere of her doubts and uncertainties, particularly about the "resurrection and afterlife". But her description of the God she has come to worship shows the reality of her faith:

> One who has more importance than we will ever recognize, one who is always open to us, although we may not always be open to him. He is forgiving, loving, at times bewildering, awe-inspiring, reassuring, yet at times disconcerting, joyful, and above all our guide, but one who will never completely be understood by us.

♦

American research asked people who had come to a church for the first time what factor brought them (apart from the "tug" of the Holy Spirit). They replied:

- ♦ 6%   the minister
- ♦ 6%   a special event at the church
- ♦ 2%   advertising
- ♦ 86% a friend or relative

However, once people were inside the church it was the preaching, the conduct of the service and, above all, the friendliness of the minster which *kept* people coming.

It is doubtful if research done in Britain would have very different results. Marcia is a good example of someone who has followed this course.

- ♦ Does your church take these facts into account?

Sheila

CHURCH SQUABBLE

In a sense I never rejected God – more a rejection of the church

Sheila was happy at her URC church until she was 17. She went regularly, taught in Sunday School, and played a full part in its life. Her life began to change when she:

had a boyfriend studying for A levels

left to work in London and started working shifts and weekends

parents went to a new church.

But the main reason was

a big split in the church and the minister left.

Sheila does not tell us the nature of the trouble but it had a profound effect upon her:

I was very positive to Christianity at that time but the problem in the church changed my outlook. It was a big turn-off at the time.

When she was 23 she was immersed in a full-time career and marriage. Then her life pattern changed:

Our daughter was born. We had not planned a child and I did not know where I was going career-wise. It was my first time at home for a long time.

I was thrilled, really happy.

This gave her time to socialize:

I went to talk to a friend up the road who I had known for a long time, I knew she was a Christian but I had not had much recent contact with her as she had left work. I would never have thought of going to church. I asked her what church she went to, for knowing what type of person Ann was, I thought it would be OK.

She asked me to go with her and I was pleasantly surprised.

It was the neighbouring Anglican church.

Through a gradual process she became a Christian, but it took her a couple of years before she felt ready to be confirmed:

> I needed to make a public declaration of faith and felt that because going to a C of E church I should commit myself to it.

The preparation consisted of eight sessions which

> started at a very basic level and the little things that you were afraid to ask were answered. The course could have been longer ... there is a need to make the course more social with more interaction.

She would have liked the course to continue after the confirmation:

> Just to get together and talk more about our own personal experiences and about our own problems.

Her husband does not go to church but she goes more than once a week:

> My faith influences everything I do – the fact that I have a personal relationship with a living God.

◆

The effect of the split in the church when Sheila was 17 made her disillusioned. After the official interview was over, she volunteered:

> Going to church is about being friends and needing to reach out to people and meet their spiritual needs ... and the spiritual needs of those who are already coming to church.

The need for love in the church was something that she kept coming back to. The impact of the division was still with her, yet how many people in the church at the time had realized the effect this was having on her or tried to help her? The church is a body of redeemed sinners, not perfected saints, and difficulties in personal relationships are bound to arise as they did in New Testament times.

♦ How can we best deal with the effect which such events have on people, especially the young and impressionable, who may well have unrealistically high expectations of what the church should be?

Sheila and many others wanted the pre-baptism/confirmation course to be longer. She appreciated the eight people in her group and going back to basics, but after her profession of faith she wanted to deal with her agenda – her experiences and problems.

♦ Do we too often expect courses to start with the Church's agenda rather than that of those who form the group?

Samantha

SAVED THROUGH AN ADVERT

I sent for a book advertised in a woman's magazine. The book was called *Power for Living*. It explained who God was and why we needed to make an actual decision for him – I read and prayed the sinner's prayer in the book and I was so overwhelmed by the love of Jesus and the fact that he accepted me as I was and forgave me all the rotten things that had ever happened in my life – I just cried and cried – seeing myself as I know the Lord must see us and yet knowing that I was totally forgiven and accepted.

Samantha was 39 when this sudden conversion happened. She had had a very nominal Christian upbringing, and had never been to church, except very occasionally in her early teens. But

other things were far more interesting. I felt the urge to go only at times like Easter.

But in her late thirties things were not going well:

My husband and I had just come out of a very rough four years – consisting of his having breakdowns, etc., but things were getting better in this respect – though I remember thinking that I didn't have much hope for the future – was this all there was?

She was

> wondering if life held anything more – I suppose I was at my rock bottom even though generally things were improving.

She became interested in spiritualism and found that their

> view was that God is love and it didn't matter what you did as long as you didn't hurt anyone – there is to them no just God. Hell to them is here – we live it out to make up for the wrongs now.

After reading the book *Power for Living* Samantha had a general sense of guilt and wept it out before God, for now she found God to be

> a righteous, just, holy, loving Father – who gives grace to the humble and who forgives our sins in repentance, who never leaves us and whose love and word endures for ever.

It was the freedom of the grace of God which captivated Samantha:

> that I was a child of God – God loved and accepted me as I was – I no longer had to be strong when I didn't feel it – I could be me with him.

Becoming a Christian meant a very great deal to her:

> I don't rely on me any more – my life belongs to the Lord – he's saved me, healed me from severe arthritis, saved my husband and I have peace and joy even though it's not easy to walk in his steps.
>
> People have asked me why I always seem happy and comment on the peaceful atmosphere in my home.

She began to go to the local Anglican church and also to a "Pentecostal/charismatic fellowship". She found that she couldn't get to the Anglican church any more

> but I knew God wanted me to join my fellowship anyway, so it would have happened sooner or later.

She and her husband were baptized after being instructed by their pastor. The service was significant for their marriage as well as for themselves as individuals:

> It was a confirmation of my faith, not only to myself but my husband who was baptized at the same time and it sealed the reality of our "new life" in Jesus. Old had gone – new was here.

◆

Samantha wrote:

> God knew me and that I was a bookworm and so to receive the *Power for Living* book was exciting. I'd built up an anticipation in waiting for it to come. It was probably the only way God could get through to me as I was at that time a very conversational person and I would have debated with any person trying to tell me about Jesus, but you can't argue with a book – you can disagree, but not argue – and God's word got through to me through any doubt I had and won.

Samantha's story of receiving a booklet and giving her life to Christ was unique among our respondents. Nevertheless, it is a good example of the power of Christian literature when properly presented. The fact that she had taken the initiative in sending for the booklet meant that there was considerable excitement in waiting for it, compared to the (lesser?) effect of something which is pushed through the letter-box. The Christian Enquiry Agency works on this principle (Inter-Church House, 35-41 Lower Marsh, London SE1 7RL).

♦ Is this something which could be used at your local level?

Hilda

UNSATISFACTORY CHURCHES

There were very few examples of people who had been much affected by their school rather than their home. The reverse was much more common. Hilda, however, had a home which she described as "no religion" and she never went to church or Sunday School. But she did go to church schools. Until she was 8 she attended a convent school and then a C of E school until 11. Her secondary school was a state school where there was "virtually no emphasis" put on the Christian faith. She says the Catholic school put "quite a lot" and the Anglican school "not much" stress on the faith.

This primary education bore fruit and she became interested in the Christian faith despite the indifference of her parents. At 12

> I started reading the Bible every night. This diminished gradually until at last I read it only occasionally.

I first started reading the Old Testament in the King James version and found it difficult. Later I read the New Testament in the King James and found it inspiring.

When I was 19 I bought myself a New English version and started to understand more.

She also found other Christian media helpful:

In my teens I read *The Imitation of Christ* and other classics such as *The Cloud of Unknowing*. I especially enjoyed *The Imitation of Christ*. When I went to university I discovered more modern books such as J I Packer's *Knowing God*.

I remember being moved to tears by *Jesus of Nazareth* on television.

Hilda married and she and her husband started going to church. But all was not well. When she was 27

I found the church (C of E) that my husband and I attended more and more depressing. At a church meeting I spoke out in anger against the way the New Testament was being discredited by the vicar (a liberal theologian). After that meeting we met a man who invited us to an evangelical fellowship where there was speaking in tongues and prayer for healing. It was a great shock to someone only used to traditional worship – however, at this man's insistence, I was prayed for to commit my life more closely to Jesus and to receive the Holy Spirit. I went home in a daze. The next day I woke up a changed person – with a voracious appetite for the Bible and to know God more. I'm 31 now and still want more of Jesus in my life.

She describes the feelings of that time. The knowledge which was central for her was

the fact that God loved *me*.

I was filled with an indescribable joy. I felt absolutely loved – and loved everybody. I had no doubts and no fears. I felt overwhelmed with gratitude to God.

This led to a change in her life and attitude:

Until that part in my life, God had been distant. I prayed to God but had never felt truly loved in a personal way. When I saw the joy in other Christians' lives – those who claimed to know him – I wanted their experience. When I heard for myself people speak in tongues and saw someone healed right before my eyes, I knew without a doubt that God loved the people in this world and worked in their lives today.

She and her husband transferred their allegiance to the House church where she had been prayed for. She was baptized "in the river!". However, attendance became difficult, since it was too far away and the services were in the evening with no crèche.

She and her husband now attend a small Methodist church. She felt "obliged" to attend an instruction course. She felt it could have been improved:

> One to one instruction would have been better. Also I felt the course was structured towards becoming a "Methodist", which I found interesting though irrelevant. Some of the group who knew little basic Christianity may have gained a little more. I would have liked a follow-up course dealing with such issues as prayer, holiness and baptism in the Spirit. I feel that not enough attention is being given to the teaching of basic Christian experience.

♦

Over four years Hilda and her husband attended three denominations and found each had their disadvantages. In her case it was the theology of one, the practical difficulties of another and the teaching method of the last.

♦ It may not be easy to find a fellowship which is able to cope with the tremendous experience which Hilda describes. Could your church? If not, why not?

♦ Should a Christian church be able to encompass all the varieties of ways in which people find God through Christ?

♦ Is Hilda right in thinking that "instruction classes" for people entering the church should concentrate on basic Christianity rather than the history of the denomination?

Pamela

THE EX-JEHOVAH'S WITNESS

Pamela went to a Presbyterian church and greatly enjoyed it until:

> I got married at 19 and moved abroad and was involved with Jehovah's Witnesses for about three years. I moved back to England and continued my involvement.

In her late twenties Pamela became disillusioned with the teaching of the Witnesses:

> I cut off from the Jehovah's Witnesses because of their God being not a loving God, I joined the United Reformed Church.

This change in her view of the being of God was crucial:

> While I was with the Witnesses God was harsh, and judgemental, and vengeful. After being with the URC God was not as bad as that, but certainly more distant than now.

But her spiritual journey was not yet over:

> Seven years after I came back from abroad I started teaching ... at a suburban middle-class school almost against my wishes ... and met a Christian person who witnessed to me. I resisted because of my experience with the JWs. Everything about the person attracted me by her character.... She used every opportunity to talk about Christianity.

Her new friend was a member of a House church:

> Through it all I was generally very happy, not depressed. I was feeling a bit "hunted" by the Christians.

She attended her new church:

> I was very moved by the music and drama activities – and the preaching as well, because everything seemed to be relevant to me. Everything seemed to be revolved around me.

However, it was not so much the services which attracted her but belonging to a "family group of nine or ten people":

> a mixed group of people who sing, talk together about personal news, pray about specific needs, pray for individual members. Sometimes a more general topic, e.g. pacifism in relation to the Gulf War.

Not all the teaching of the church was attractive to her:

> I wasn't very happy with the belief of the man being the "boss" of the family.

She was baptized:

> I'd given my life to the Lord and at first I didn't feel the need to be baptized. Gradually started thinking it was the right thing to do.

However, the baptism was a rather disappointing experience. Pamela described it as "not very worthwhile":

> I was hoping my husband would be challenged and make some response but he didn't.

But the basic teaching about the unconditional love of God was the main message she heard from the church:

> I feel that I've got closer to God through understanding he wants a relationship with me. That God wants a relationship with me in major things and I am aware that he loves me so much just as I am.

At the heart of Pamela's spiritual journey was the search for a church which spoke of a God of love. The developing "image" or "icon" of God was found to be an essential part of being evangelized.

    ◆ Do we explain the character of God to people enough?

Many of our respondents echoed the words of Pamela: "He loves me so much just as I am."

Pamela found the most significant part of her new church was the house group.

> ♦ Do we see this as something to introduce people into as soon as possible after they join the church, or is it something which is mentioned only to "mature" Christians? Are any house groups in your church geared up to welcoming new people and adjusting their programmes to make this possible – easier material for discussion ... no use of jargon ... no in-group jokes?

It is sometimes thought that Jehovah's Witnesses, Mormons, etc. are difficult to evangelize. It is significant that more than 2 per cent of our respondents said that they had previously belonged to one of these groups. Most of them spoke of rigid and unbending teaching, and, like Pamela, a view of God which did not agree with that of the New Testament.

> ♦ Are you prepared to witness calmly, gently and winsomely to the loving God and father of our Lord Jesus Christ?

Arthur

THANKFULNESS

Arthur was 45 when:

> both our marriages broke down. Then we met and moved in together.

Arthur then remarried after which

> My [new] wife then had a very bad accident and escaped very lightly and we both felt the need to thank God so we went to church. Together we came to Christ.

The vicar and his wife were the most significant part of this process:

> They got to know us very quickly and they blessed our marriage which had quite an effect on us. They are always prepared to listen to us. We have tremendous conversations and they are always ready to put themselves out for their congregation.

Arthur recognizes that:

> I was looking for something else in my life.

Perhaps this went back to his childhood. He had been brought up by his grandparents and went regularly to church with his grandfather. At the age of 14 he stopped:

> I don't really know why ... I never had any problem going to church.

This was not the experience he had when he returned to church although he had come to realize "what fun it could be" (the church was described as "ecumenical"):

> Initially we found a "them" and "us" situation and we didn't know anyone. It wasn't until we went along to one or two social events that we felt more relaxed.

His journey to faith was aided by a mission they had attended, though the main factor which Arthur thinks led to his new-found faith was his friendship with the vicar and his wife. His confirmation a few months before had also been "very moving".

He is very conscious that he is still working at his faith. When asked "What does being a Christian mean to you personally?" he answered:

> I suppose trying to live my life in the Lord. Being more considerate of others. I am a very new Christian, in at the deep end and learning very quickly. I try to be as the Lord would want me to be ... "to be good".

As an accountant:

> I find working in a non-Christian place of work difficult.

◆

Quite a number of the respondents mentioned "thanksgiving" as a factor which brought them to God. While his wife's recovery from illness was one of the main reasons, it may well be that Arthur and his new wife were also giving thanks for a period of tranquillity after what must have been a time of great upheaval for both of them.

♦ Do our churches give non-churchgoers an opportunity for giving thanks?

When *Finding Faith Today* was first published, the press and broadcasting programmes gave much space to the finding that "evangelistic events" were mentioned as the "main" factor involved in people coming to Christ by only 4 per cent of the respondents, despite the fact that similar figures had been given by other researchers. They ignored the fact that *Finding Faith Today* also said that evangelistic events were said to be a supporting factor by 13 per cent of the people interviewed. In other words these events may not bring many to faith, but they do confirm the faith of a considerably larger number of people, like Arthur.

> ♦ Do we look to evangelistic events for the wrong reason i.e. to bring people to faith rather than encouraging new Christians in their faith? If this is so, do we need to accept with more joy than normal the frequently given evaluation after such an event: "It did not bring in many people from outside but it certainly did the church a power of good"?

Joyce

BEYOND PREJUDICE

Joyce is 37. She had a sudden conversion on 20 March 1989. Her story is like that of many others to whom the Christian faith comes quickly.

She went to a Church of England Sunday School and loved it. Then, at the age of 12 "interest had gone".

> My mother gave me the choice. I wasn't getting anything out of it, so decided not to go. No attendance at adult church services.

She never went to church again, never prayed, never read her Bible. God

> was somebody who was all right for other people but who wasn't there for me.

Then, when she was 36, her mother was very ill. Her mother was usually "strong, but now she felt she did not know what to do, which disturbed me".

> I'd asked lots of questions of a Christian friend. I gave my life to the Lord, but didn't realize fully what I'd done until discussing things with another two Christian friends at a Bible study two weeks later.

She joined a Christian Fellowship:

> I chose the church I go to through the Christian friends I'd already got going there.

She found it "very difficult", despite the help she received from her friends. She had some prejudices to overcome:

> What are that strange lot? I presumed they were different. I didn't know what to expect ... it was different to anything I'd been to before – then I found that was the experience of others in the group initially too.

She was later baptized:

> because although you've possibly committed yourself to Christ previously, it really confirmed it doing it before the church – and it washes away your sin. I felt then that I really knew Christ: I'd met him – he wasn't still on the cross.

The baptism partly cleared up for Joyce a problem she had had for some time – that

> Christ had died for us. I couldn't get Christ off the cross – and I still struggle with that sometimes.

Life is not always easy for Joyce. Although within herself

> I'm happier, more aware of situations around me. I always see good in everyone and never see bad.

Her close family are not supportive (and Joyce says that this prevents her going to church as often as she would like):

> My mother-in-law says she can't have the same conversations with me, and initially she felt she was losing me. My husband says I'm a "goody-goody" now.

♦

Joyce's two friends at the Bible study were able to explain to her what had happened when she gave her life to the Lord.

> ♦ Do we see this as a significant way of helping people – giving them an understanding of what God has done for them? It is an awesome responsibility if we get it wrong …

Joyce says that she had no preparation before her baptism. This is something which is not uncommon in the new churches.

> ♦ Would it have been helpful if she had had an opportunity of talking through the very real theological difficulty she had about the cross, and encouraging her to see Christ risen and triumphant as well?

Emma

JOURNEY THROUGH THE DENOMINATIONS

Emma gives us a very full picture of her spiritual journey. It has taken her through several traditions and many years. She was 50 when we spoke to her.
Her faith means

> an awful lot of things – having Jesus in my life and the Holy Spirit, having God as my Father, having someone to turn to and share things with, whatever happens – good or bad. I don't feel better than anyone else, but have a different dimension in my life – everything that happens relates to me being a Christian – everything is sacred.

Emma started with "no religion".

Her parents were hostile. She never went to church or Sunday School. Her primary school did nothing to help her spiritually. Even when Emma was a member of the Brownies and Guides she did not go to the church parade.

However, Emma was one of the very few of our respondents who found her secondary school helpful:

> The Scripture teacher at school influenced me – though I resisted because of my upbringing. I was already reading the Bible – she made it fascinating – the way she told the stories. She encouraged me to stop fighting my interest and be more positive. I needed space to reject my upbringing.

She had never read the Bible as a youngster. Now in her teens, she found it "fascinating" and later "inspiring" and "comforting":

> I saw a pattern in it. I read the Old Testament more than the New and saw the prophetic side of Jesus – how the Old and the New fitted together. It all clicked – that Jesus was the Lamb of God – the prophets foretold an event beyond their own circumstances. Theologically, that had much influence.

A group of Christian friends also helped her by "befriending me in a way no one had before".

Over a period of two years, and while in her mid-teens, Emma became a Christian. Like most of our respondents she was not going through any crisis:

> I was just looking forward to my O levels! I wasn't concerned or anxious. I was my normal, flippant, happy-go-lucky self.

It was the love of God which touched her:

> He didn't just love us *en masse*, but I could have a *personal* relationship with him. If I'd been the only person in the world he would have died for me.

> He's so holy – not so much of a schoolmaster as I'd thought – not looking at me with such disdain. Now it doesn't matter what I have done, do, and will do, provided I don't want to hurt him.... He's more tolerant than I'd thought.

Emma started to go to church – and over the years visited various denominations – Anglican, Baptist and Pentecostal. Now she is a Roman Catholic.

When she was 29 she had a "charismatic experience":

> I had an infilling of the Holy Spirit for the first time – and I was healed at the same time. It was almost repeated when I was confirmed into the Roman Catholic church last year. I spoke in tongues – I felt a peace, almost an excess of peace! I don't know how else to describe it. There was nothing violent – no shaking or sudden rush – it was almost an

> overwhelming sense of peace and wellbeing: the presence of God. It wasn't spectacular, but very meaningful. People noticed me "glowing" the next day ... I wasn't aware that I was.

This was not an experience she had expected. Quite the reverse:

> It taught me a lesson about intolerance – I'd been very anti-people who talked about such experiences. God showed me that I shouldn't judge others' experiences, that one could interpret Scripture wrongly. It taught me that God loved me and made me less argumentative. People said I was easier to live with and was more sunny, bright and cheerful. It didn't make me any less a sinner – but changed my attitude without me particularly realizing. I responded to God as he seemed almost to over-compensate. He came to me far more than I reached out to him. He seemed so generous.

During these years her faith meant much to her:

> I think I'd be part of the rat race if I hadn't become a Christian – being more selfish, wanting everything for me ... I might have got to the top of my profession but been extremely lonely.

Her journey into the Catholic church was many years later, when she was in her late forties:

> I felt I wanted to belong to a church seeming to be Catholic – and to be universal in the sense of all over the world, worshipping with the same intention.

> I think I would have been Catholic from the beginning if I'd been introduced to it, but was put off it by evangelical Christians. I am still regarded as needing to be rescued by some of them – it's very sad.... The Incarnation has become more meaningful to me. The separation of secular and sacred was an emphasis and attitude I felt rejected by in what I feel is my calling.

Her confirmation was very worthwhile:

> I experienced the Holy Spirit in it, commissioning me in a new way. I felt that I was beginning something new for God. He was giving me power and strength to go and do it. A wonderful, special way of entering a church: it's scriptural too – anointing and laying on of hands.

The church was seen as a very important part of her life:

> We're part of a body and need to meet with other parts! Recognizing Jesus as the head, we need to relate to him as individuals and to one another, and to him collectively.

♦

Emma demonstrates a common modern phenomenon. Her home had no particular denominational allegiance and so she had no sense of loyalty to one denomination. She moved easily between churches, looking for fellowship and a widening of her spiritual horizons. For all we know she may move to another denomination if it appears more satisfactory for her. (A recent survey of a number of lay people in an Anglican diocese showed that almost 60 per cent had no, or very little, church upbringing, 21 per cent had been brought up as Anglicans, 5 per cent as Roman Catholics and 15 per cent as other denominations.)

We found that 20 per cent of the people surveyed had changed their denomination during the comparatively short time leading up to their profession of faith.

> ♦ How many in our own congregation are from different denominational roots? Do we make allowances for this, or do we assume that they understand our language and history?

Emma was particularly unhappy about the emphasis in her previous church about "the separation between secular and sacred" which she felt was wrong. While there is much in the New Testament, particularly in John's Gospel about being separate from the world, Christians are also the followers of someone who was accused of being a friend of winebibbers, sinners and prostitutes and who went into disreputable places.

> ♦ What guidance can we give to others (and ourselves) about this?

Yvonne

THE VISION

I had a lot of problems. Approximately thirteen years ago I got married and came to live here – I wanted a child but was unable to conceive. I took it personally and it resulted in me taking a massive overdose.

She describes what happened:

I had a vision after taking the overdose. I lay in hospital with everyone running around me and I felt this real calmness and a vision of a "being" came to me and said, "I'm not ready for you yet Yvonne; I'll call you when it's time."

It was that sudden vision which Yvonne looks back on as the time when she became a Christian, though it was a long time before this led to her going to church or making a public commitment:

The vision made me think a lot about God's existence.

From then on I've been thinking about God. Then, my father had a stroke, he is now terminally ill, and I wondered why. I also had five miscarriages. I had one child, then five miscarriages in between. Eventually I had a second child. Things picked up – but I became pregnant again and I wasn't very happy about it. At the same time I sustained a back injury – over which I was on my back for thirteen weeks. Didn't know where I was going in life. Then I heard about the "basics course" at the Vicarage. I went to that, and by going through the Bible and meeting other people who'd had problems, I had a wonderful feeling that I wasn't alone and someone was there listening to me. In consequence I asked Christ to come into my life.

Yvonne describes her state of mind at the time as "normal". While she looked back to the "vision" as the main factor in bringing her to faith, she said the influence of her vicar was the main supporting factor:

He listened to everything I'd got to say and explained all that I didn't understand and taught me to "love me" really.

Starting going to church she described as "very easy" – though there were some cultural difficulties ...

> I feel that that's God's home and now I've stood up and professed to be a Christian I've got a damn good right to be there. I say that because there are some at church – older, who claim to have been Christians for years and tend to regard the newcomers as intruders. Not just older, though, but people who've always gone to church, even of my own age group.

There was a difference in her life.

> I feel so much more at ease with life and people. I have an inner peace. It's just good to be alive with Jesus Christ.

Though her relatives found it hard to come to terms with the new Yvonne:

> my mum thinks I'm more in control and I don't shout as much, but thinks it's rather weird when I say, "I've got God on my side now."

> My husband thinks it's strange that I've got a prayer book by the bedside rather than a novel, but he thinks I'm a more peaceful person and seem to cope with problems better.

Yvonne had been baptized as a Methodist and gone reasonably regularly to Sunday School until the age of 15:

> I started working and met people who weren't church orientated, met boys, etc. I'd started attending church by then and it seemed pretty boring for that age.

When she was 33, after the basics course, she was confirmed as an Anglican:

> It was the next step to take and something to shout about to everyone! It put my feelings into action.

◆

Most of the people interviewed described the reception they found at church as "friendly". However, there were some, like Yvonne, who had encountered antagonism. One suspects that she is not easily put down and had made her feelings heard. It can happen that some within a congregation are genuinely warm and friendly when a new person comes to church but are less so when the newcomers seem to be suggesting changes or challenging other people's positions.

   ♦ Is this true in your church?

Norma

A GRADUAL CONVERSION

One of the most important findings of the research project was the proportion of people who saw their entry into the Christian faith as being a sudden event and those who saw it as a gradual unfolding of God, leading up to a public profession of faith. Norma saw herself as beginning a gradual process at the age of 20 which was still continuing 22 years later.

   She said that the most important factor in bringing her to faith was her parents. This was not a common response from somebody of her age. Most of the people who cited their home as being important were under 25. It is still more surprising in that

> I always felt sad that my Dad wouldn't let me be confirmed when I was 11 years old; I felt I wanted to do it for the right reasons.

While her parents were reasonably positive about her going to Sunday School, they did not go to church themselves at that time (her mother went later), and she described them as being "of no particular denomination". She stopped going to church when she was 13:

> People laughed at you for going to church – very influenced at that age by peers.

However, she looked back on their positive attitude to the Christian faith as being the main factor in her declaration of faith:

> they guided me from childhood: I came to think that they were right and I followed them.

In her twenties, a series of events happened:

> When mother began her illness it was a shock to see her, and I prayed a lot for her.... Husband's mother died suddenly.... I had a miscarriage.... All these things I didn't understand (ten-year period of searching for reasons).

If there was a point at which she became more aware of God it was when ...

> I opened myself to him when my daughter was born and a greater closeness to God grew from then.

Looking back on her life she now says that while she had always been a Christian, that was the time when she became more committed.

It was a good many years later that she herself began to go to church with any frequency although she had always gone to church "several times a year". It was due to her children's pressure:

> my children were taken by my mother and then they asked me why I didn't go. I felt guilty and felt better when I did go.

(It was interesting to see the influence that Norma's mother had in the whole process. While not being a churchgoer herself, she was a prime agent in bringing Norma and her family to God.)

What did she find when she got to church? The first was the social environment:

> I knew so many people who were parents of my children's schoolfriends.

However, this was not entirely helpful.

> I felt that some of these people were more committed but I couldn't handle these people praying together and I didn't want to be taken over. They seemed too familiar and treated God quite casually.

She also found

> A very entertaining vicar who held your interest. I could understand what he said and could associate with what he says.

It was still many years before Norma felt ready to be confirmed, although she always felt that she wanted to be:

> My daughter was being confirmed and I felt at every communion that I hadn't done what I should have done.

Despite this step of commitment Norma still feels herself rather on the outside of the church. She is probably right in saying that her journey to faith is not yet over. She goes to church "two or three times a month", which is less than most of the people who took part in the survey. As she says, she is "not very involved" in the life of the church. The gradual process still goes on.

◆

♦ Are there times when long-time members of the church are too familiar with God which frightens those who are not used to our particular church culture? Norma's reactions when she first started to come to church more regularly suggests that they seemed to her to be over-intense and off-putting.

Once again we find the two elements which help people to come to church – a social setting in which they feel at ease and a minister to whom they can relate. Usually it comes in that order. It may be that people cannot relate to the "person at the front" until they feel at their ease.

The points Norma mentions which helped her towards faith were:

♦ the spate of illnesses which her family had when she was in her twenties

♦ the sense of God at the birth of her daughter

♦ the "Why don't you come to church?" questions of her daughter when she was taken to Sunday School

♦ the confirmation of her daughter which challenged her to be confirmed herself – thirty years after she had first wanted to be!

But she still does not feel completely "converted" and part of the church.

♦ Can you identify with this very gradual process and the sense of looking in from the outside which Norma still has? Is it like your journey or the journey of someone you know?

Stephen

THE CHOIR BOY

Very few of our respondents spoke of belonging to a church choir when they were young. Some might say cynically that churchgoing had put them off for life!

Stephen regularly sang in the Anglican church choir from the age of 12 to 17:

> In a sense I went because of the choir. I did not look forward to the church itself ... it had no effect on what I believed.

There was something deeper which Stephen was looking for:

> I went to an early communion once a month (which had nothing to do with choir) and I did take that seriously.

Another influence was at work on Stephen during these years – his church secondary school:

> There was a chaplain who impressed me a lot. The church was "high" – the school was "low". I didn't realize the difference.

He started to read the gospels and found them "fascinating".

Then life changed. He went to college and stopped going to church "other than to something special during the holidays".

He later described himself as an "agnostic":

> I rejected the religion I was brought up in. I didn't think anything much about God at all.

He became a historian, and it was through his work that he came to faith. He was in his late thirties:

> I found myself coming across the Christian aspects of the arts (including art and architecture). A gradual immersion in all these and realizing there is something more important underlying it.

His view of God expanded:

> It is difficult to explain but I think of God as something inside me, the deepest thing that I am, and something outside me which includes every absolute (like truth, beauty, and so on).

His doubts still surface at times:

> I do sometimes wonder if the whole thing is true, but essentially there are things I'm sure of which I can hold on to.

In particular

> parts of the New Testament seem to have a great sense of conviction, such as parts of St John and the resurrection stories.

His denominational allegiance went through several changes. About six years ago he and his wife went to Rome. Stephen looks back on this visit as having great significance:

> We went to the Pope's Whit Sunday address and were conscious of a "supernatural" atmosphere – perhaps the result of all those people.

Spiritually things began to make sense:

> The Rome thing and others acted as catalysts. I had an inkling of the love of God as being something that could counteract evil. Once I could believe in "evil" I could also believe the converse, and that "good" could conquer it.

After that Stephen started going infrequently to a Roman Catholic church.

> I talked to an RC priest and was confused about where I was going. I decided I belonged to the C of E – returning to my roots.

After attending the Anglican church

> I came to think that the C of E was just as good – but then began to feel that was wrong. For me the RC church seemed the best version of the church. The RCs seemed more universal, widely spread.

As a result he attended the local Catholic church and went through twenty or more sessions of the RCIA.

> The instruction was useful, but there was also a feeling of being drawn into the church – the people were very welcoming so it was more than just teaching.

He does not see himself as being much involved in the life of the church, but is not happy about this. He is

> trying to decide what level of involvement [he should have].

He finds the Bible very important and reads it daily.
His wife was opposed to his churchgoing, but later joined him and now

> There's a difference in the way we spend our time and money. I'm conscious there's a difference in the way I think about and approach things. It's all in the light of Christianity.

♦

Stephen was unusual in finding God through his love of art and history. Nearly everybody else we questioned found God through seeing the lives of other Christians rather than their creative work. Yet in Britain we have an enormous Christian heritage:

> ♦ architecture – churches, chapels, cathedrals
>
> ♦ art – galleries full of Christian stories: the visual aids of the past painted by Christians
>
> ♦ music – both classical music and modern material produced by Christian people which sets out a Christian view of the world.

There is also a less obvious heritage – the keeping of Sunday as a special day, the Christian faith being taught in schools, charitable status for churches. Much of this is being rapidly eroded but much still remains.

> ♦ How can we make the fullest use of these opportunities to point people to the Christ who is behind our Christian heritage?

EPILOGUE

Doing your own research into faith journeys

Various people need to know the faith journeys of those around them:

Church leaders – in order to:

♦ find out the spiritual background of those in their congregation. Too often they assume they know it but in fact know only a small part (usually the bit they had a hand in). We may well find that we understand better why some people react the way they do when we know their faith journey.

♦ have a strategy for evangelism. Particularly important is to know the faith journeys of those who have recently joined the church. If the Holy Spirit often blows in one direction by bringing people to faith by one method, we would do well to follow along the lines he has set us. For example, if we find that preaching is being used, there is a need to make the fullest use of the opportunities leaders have. If we find a particular evangelistic method is being used, then we need to concentrate upon it. If we find that friendship is the main method (and we probably shall if *Finding Faith Today* is anything to go by), then we need to give the congregation self-confidence to share their faith.

House group members – in order to:

♦ help them to share with other members of the group what their own faith journey has been, and so build confidence in faith-sharing.

♦ teach them that not everyone has come to faith in the same way as themselves and the multi-faceted and wonderful ways in which God works

♦ show how helpful research of this nature is.

Do not be shy of engaging in this sort of research because it is helpful to the people who are being interviewed. It may well be the first time they have ever had a chance of seeing systematically how God has worked throughout their life. To be able to trace the golden thread of his purposes can give them a sense of his providence, just as the people of Israel are reminded over and over again in the Old Testament of the "God who led...". God is a God of our personal history as well as of all history.

◆

One of the most intensive religious projects was that which produced *Finding Faith Today*. This is what was learnt.

Research of this kind is *not*

◆ a jumble of anecdotes. The Christian world has been plagued by poor research and too many evangelistic methods have been founded on a few good stories.

◆ of universal significance. It may tell you much about what God is doing in your area, but it cannot be extrapolated unless you have far more examples than a local church is likely to provide. The statisticians told us when we were preparing to do the FFT research that we needed to get at least 400 samples taken at random over the country and in every denomination (in the end we had 511 respondents).

◆ an excuse for prying into people's lives. If they want to take part well and good, but confidentiality must be maintained. This means that church leaders are unlikely to be able to use in public the stories of people in their congregation since they will probably be recognizable – unless, of course, they get the permission of the person or people concerned beforehand. In a book like this, confidentiality is not difficult. We can alter a few names and omit a few facts which might pinpoint a person or a church. It is less easy on a local scale. The assurance of confidentiality is essential, otherwise people will not talk of their experiences of God.

◆ to be done lightly. It is too easy to interview people and forget that the hard work is drawing the conclusions afterwards. Someone who is skilled in analysing questionnaires and putting the results on to a computer is valuable but not essential. If research is not carried through the respondents, who have either given their time to be interviewed or completed a questionnaire, they will feel short-changed.

◆ about us speaking to people but about *listening* to them. It does not matter what we think about what they say – accept whether or not it is theologically or grammatically correct. One question in particular needs to be guarded against – some theologies long to find a "moment of conversion" – when someone "becomes a Christian". As the *Finding Faith Today* research showed, many people cannot point to such a moment and that viewpoint has to be respected. We must not try to invent one for our own satisfaction to fit our plans.

Methods of research

Some researchers feel that questionnaires are old hat and use group enquiries, story telling and more arcane methods. However, these need a great deal of skill because there is a considerable subjective element within them.

One of the most difficult parts of research is to cut out the influence of the researcher. For this reason researchers in the street tend to use a deadpan face and ask questions in a monotone. The way questions are asked (either face to face or on paper) can be crucial.

The creation of a questionnaire is no easy task. In doing the *Finding Faith Today* research we designed the questionnaire, sent it round to various people for criticism, changed it, piloted it with about 20 people, then changed it again. We had endless discussions about the use of words. For example, "conversion" in most people's minds is essentially a sudden event, so what should we use instead? Even then we got it wrong. We wanted to find out if people had changed their denominational allegiance as a result of their "conversion" and so we asked "Have you changed your church?" forgetting that "church" can mean either denomination or local church. Probably the best way of undertaking this at local level is to get hold of a copy of the *Technical Report on Finding Faith Today* available from Bible Society. This includes all the questionnaires we used and the full results of the research. It was written by our researcher, Pam Hanley, and is a model of its kind.

Questionnaires – face to face or written?

There are negatives and positives to both:

♦ Face to face is warmer and more friendly, but the personality of the interviewer can intrude and people are often more shy of discussing something personal in front of someone else. There is also a risk of someone answering in the way they think their interviewer wants them to rather than speaking the truth. This is often seen in answers to questions such as "How often do you read your Bible?"

♦ Written answers are more impersonal, but they often give the sense of confidentiality which enables people to be free to share their experiences. On the other hand, they may cause problems for people who are not well-educated and find writing difficult or impossible. (Reading through the *Finding Faith Today* responses it was clear that many people wrote with considerable difficulty, and often produced some of the most striking phrases and descriptions – as you can see earlier in this book.) It is sometimes thought that people will not tell stories if they have to write them down. We did not find this to be so.

When doing the FFT research we were surprised by the quality of the written responses. Obviously those who were illiterate had to be interviewed face to face, but many people had obviously taken a great deal of time and effort to fill in their questionnaires.

♦

The questionnaire

Before starting to compose the questionnaire it is essential that you write down the questions to which you want responses. While you probably will not want to do as extensive a questionnaire as *Finding Faith Today*, you may like to pick and choose from the questions we were seeking to answer (I have put a * against those we found particularly important).

Personal background

What is your age ... sex ... sociological level ... education ... ethnic background ... type of employment?*

Past Christian experience

Your childhood: what was the attitude to religion in your home?*

If Christian, what denomination?

Did you attend church/Sunday School. If so, did you like it? If you left it – why and when?*

Did you have any contact with para-church bodies, youth organizations, etc. If so, what effect did they have?

Did school influence your faith, or lack of it?*

If you read the Bible, what did you make of it?

Was any other book, film, etc. helpful?

Were there people who influenced you spiritually?

Leading up to their profession of faith.

Have you been conscious of a "spiritual journey"?*

Did you have a "turning to God"? Was it sudden or gradual?*

Were you going through some crisis at this time?

Did you have any sense of guilt or sin?*

Were there any "unusual occurrences"?*

Was there any sense of "the presence of God"?

Did your "image" of God change?*

What part of the Christian message did you find hard to believe? What part was most attractive to you?

What change took place:

> in your attitude to life *
> in relating to others?
> in the way you spent your time?
> in your attitude to the Church and Christian people?*

What were the main factors which brought you to the place of "turning"?*

What part did the church play in this? If so, what was attractive ... difficult?*

Has there been any change in denominational allegiance? If so, why?

The public rite of initiation

What teaching was given? How did you rate it?*

How helpful was the initiation rite itself?

What support did you get from family and friends?

What continuing Christian education did you receive afterwards?

You may well find that you want to ask more questions, but be aware of the rule of thumb which says that no interview should last more than an hour or people's concentration flags. We had a further list of eleven questions we would have liked to ask about personality, political persuasion, primary loyalty, emotional release, etc., but felt that they would overburden our respondents. It is important to distinguish between trying to answer questions which have interesting answers and those which are genuinely useful to our evangelism.

The *Finding Faith Today* questionnaire was 22 pages long and was usually completed in about an hour.

Producing the Results

This is often the most difficult and time-consuming part of any research and it needs to be planned from the beginning. Reading through the questionnaires ... putting the answers on to computer or making full notes ... beginning to produce answers to the questions you wanted answered ... checking and rechecking. Short cuts here produce poor research, and consequently wobbly strategy.

Also available from Bible Society:

Finding Faith Today

John Finney's original report based on research carried out by Pam Hanley and Bible Society on behalf of Churches Together in England.

Journeys into Faith

A group study resource based on the research of *Finding Faith Today* by John Young, Diocesan Evangelist for the Diocese of York.

The Technical Report on *Finding Faith Today*

Written by Pam Hanley at the end of her research, giving in greater detail the statistical findings of *Finding Faith Today*.